A

BICYCLIST'S GUIDE
TO
BAY AREA HISTORY

Carol O'Hare

Fair Oaks Publishing Co.
Sunnyvale, California

Design and maps by Susan Cronin-Paris

Published by Fair Oaks Publishing Company
941 Populus Place, Sunnyvale, CA 94086
(408) 732-1078

Library Of Congress Cataloging - in - Publication Data

O'Hare, Carol
        A bicyclist's guide to Bay Area history / by Carol O'Hare. —
Rev. ed.
    p.   cm.
    ISBN 0-933271-03-4
    1. Bicycle touring—California—San Francisco Bay Area—Guidebooks.
    2. San Francisco Bay Area (Calif.)—Description and travel—
    I. Title.
    GV1045.5.C22S266   1989
    917.94'6—dc19   89-1298
                                                           CIP

Table of Contents

Introduction

When I first moved to California from the East Coast, I was convinced that the West had little to offer in the way of real history. But as I began to explore my adopted state, I quickly learned how wrong I was. The San Francisco Bay Area especially has a unique charm that includes a fascinating variety of historic sites. And I have also discovered one of the best ways to enjoy these explorations is from the seat of a bicycle.

Sightseeing by bicycle can present problems, however. More than once my husband and I have wandered around in unfamiliar territory, seeking some old building we had read about, only to never locate it at all, or to discover it was not worth the effort once we did. We have also found ourselves on heavily congested roads not safe for cycling, in shadeless areas on a hot summer day, or exhausted when a ride turned out to be more strenuous than we had anticipated. *A Bicyclist's Guide to Bay Area History* was written to share what we have learned from these experiences. In this second edition of the book, I have added several new rides and revised others. My goal, however, remains unchanged—to guide you to the interesting historic sites that abound throughout the Bay Area, while also providing you with a pleasant day of cycling.

How to use this book: The 18 rides described here vary greatly in length and difficulty. Some are short and easy, suitable for an afternoon family outing. Others offer the distance and challenge sought by more experienced cyclists. Many have optional side trips, which add mileage and oftentimes more difficult conditions, making these tours appropriate for riders of varying ability levels.

The ratings I have given the rides are, of course, subjective. They take into account mileage, terrain, road conditions and traffic situations. Generally, an **easy** ride is short, flat, follows bike lanes or roads with adequate shoulder, and avoids heavy traffic. A **strenuous** ride, on the other hand, is longer, usually includes demanding hill climbing, may be on rough roads with no shoulder, and sometimes involves heavy traffic. **Moderate** and **moderately strenuous** rides fall in between. I have tried to provide enough descriptive detail about each tour to allow you to choose those rides that will suit you best.

The distances given are not meant to be exact, but to tell you approximately how many miles each ride is, how far it is to the next turn or stopping point, and how long the hill ahead of you is going to be. You may find that these excursions take up to twice as long as you might expect from the stated mileage, since you will be stopping frequently. Be sure to allow plenty of time for checking directions, enjoying the scenery and visiting historic sites.

The itineraries themselves were designed to include the most interesting of the historic places in each area, while following the safest and most enjoyable cycling routes. As a result, some of them are rather complicated, especially in urban areas. You will need to refer to the text for complete directions, rather than rely on the maps alone.

In addition to route descriptions and historical lore, I have included the location of several campgrounds and hostels, should you wish to plan an overnight stay. Museums of interest and their hours are also noted, as well as places to buy food and use the restroom. My aim has been to furnish all the information you will need to plan a pleasurable outing.

The facts presented here were checked for accuracy just before the book went to press. But museum hours and telephone numbers change, road surfaces may improve or deteriorate. Occasionally, even buildings are torn down or moved. If you find any errors or changes, please write me, so I can correct them in the next printing.

Before setting out, make sure your bicycle is in good working order and that you are prepared to fix a flat. Nothing spoils a ride more quickly than getting caught with a broken-down bike, miles from your car. You may want to bring along a lock, so you can visit places of interest without worrying about the safety of your equipment. Helmets are strongly recommended for *your* safety. Since many of the buildings described here are not public property, please respect the privacy of the occupants. And don't forget to obey the traffic laws. This is even more important in light of the increasing numbers of automobiles and bicycles sharing the road.

Although written for bicyclists, this book can also be used by those who wish to make the tours by car (except for the occasional sections on bike paths). Parts of the routes may also be comfortably covered on foot. No matter what your mode of transportation, have a pleasant and safe journey, as you explore the delights of Bay Area history.

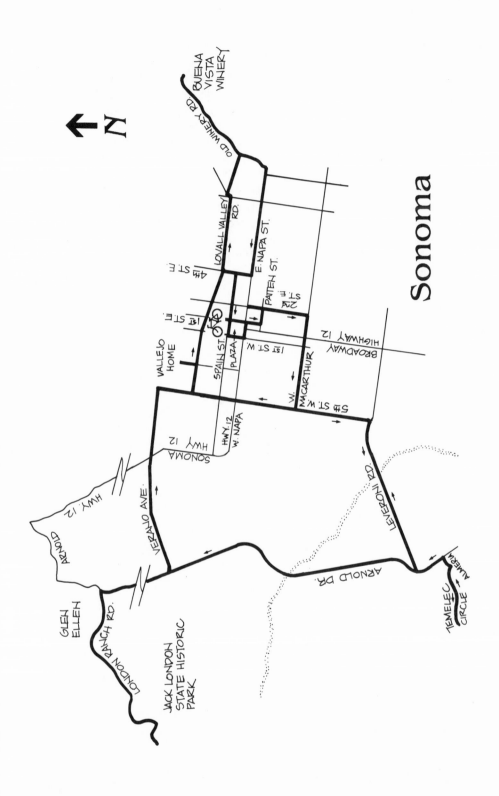

Sonoma

Sonoma

Distance: 10 or 13.5 miles with 16.5 mile optional side trip

Rating: The shorter rides are **easy**, following flat city streets and country roads. Traffic may be heavy near the Plaza, especially on weekend afternoons. The optional side trip to Glen Ellen is **moderately strenuous**, with a challenging mile-long climb to Jack London State Historic Park. There are also some stretches of narrow, rough road with no shoulder and fast-moving traffic along the way. Summer weather in Sonoma is hot and dry, perfect for grape-growing, but potentially hard on bicyclists. All other seasons are fine for this fascinating ride.

Highlights: Sonoma, in the heart of the wine country, is among the most historic towns in the state. It is the location of the last established mission, site of the founding of the "Republic of California" by the Bear Flag Party, and home of General Mariano Vallejo, one of the most important and influential men of his time. Many of the old buildings around the Plaza have been well preserved and are open to the public. The tour also includes two long-established wineries. The high point of the Glen Ellen trip is visiting the early 20th century homes of author Jack London.

Begin your ride at the Plaza, in the center of Sonoma. The Plaza is located on Highway 12, the road that brings you into town. There is free parking behind the State Historic Park on the north side of the Plaza, off First Street East. Be sure to allow plenty of time to explore the Plaza and its historic buildings, as there is much to see here.

Start at the Mission San Francisco Solano, on the corner of First Street East and East Spain Street. The **Sonoma Mission**, as it is commonly called, was founded in 1823, the last and most northerly of the 21 missions. It was established not only to Christianize the Indians, but also to discourage further expansion by the Russians who had settlements at Fort Ross and Bodega.

The only remaining building of the original complex is the long, low adobe wing used as the padres' living quarters. Constructed in 1825, it is the oldest building in Sonoma. The present small chapel was erected by General Vallejo in 1840 as a parish church. After 1881 it was used as a hay barn, winery and blacksmith shop before becoming state property in 1903. The mission buildings are now part of the State Historic Park, open daily from 10:00 am to 5:00 pm. The small admission charge also covers several other state-owned buildings.

Sonoma Mission

On the other side of First Street, facing the Plaza, is the **Sonoma Barracks**, a restored two-story adobe. It was built between 1836 and 1840 by Indian laborers to house Mexican army troops under the command of General Vallejo. The troops first arrived in 1834 when Vallejo, then the Commandant of the Presidio at San Francisco, was instructed to establish a garrison and town here.

The building also served as the capitol of the California Republic during the Bear Flag Revolt and housed the U.S. Army during the 1850's. Now part of the Historic Park, the barracks contain an informative museum telling the stories of the Indian, Mexican and American periods in Sonoma history.

Ride south on First Street East to circle the Plaza. (If traffic is heavy, however, or if you wish to spend more time examining the buildings surrounding the Plaza, you may decide to lock your bicycle and do this part of the tour on foot.)

The **Sonoma Plaza**, the largest of its kind in California, was laid out in 1834 by General Vallejo with the help of Captain William Richardson. Using a pocket compass, they also surveyed the streets for the mile square town and divided them into lots.

The Plaza has seen many uses over the years. Mexican and Indian soldiers drilled on it in the late 1830's. Horse races and duels were held here. Soil from the Plaza was used to make adobe bricks for the buildings surrounding it. By the 1870's, the Plaza was bare of trees, and livestock of all kinds had grazed and trampled the ground. In the 1880's the Sonoma Valley Railroad covered half of this open space with tracks, coal yard, depot, car barn and other railroad buildings.

The first step in beautifying the Plaza came in 1890, when a law suit forced the railroad to remove its equipment. Several years later, landscaping by the Ladies Improvement Club resulted in the present parklike setting. Today, the Plaza contains hundreds of trees and shrubs, a rose garden, duck pond, playground, picnic tables, restrooms, and the City Hall.

The Plaza was also the scene of one of the more colorful events in California history. In the 1840's large numbers of Americans arrived in California, lured by rumors of free land. Met by restrictions that prohibited them from owning land and fearful of being driven out of California by the Mexican government, a group of settlers decided to take matters into their own hands. On June 14, 1846, with the unofficial backing of Captain John C. Fremont, they captured the unresisting Pueblo of Sonoma and arrested Vallejo. Even though Vallejo supported annexation of California by the United States, he was imprisoned for two months at Sutter's Fort.

The Americans announced the establishment of a free and independent Republic of California and raised a homemade flag—the Bear Flag—over Sonoma. Less than a month later it was replaced by that of the United States, after the Mexican capital at Monterey was captured. The revolt, unfortunately, prevented the peaceful annexation of California by the United States and made war with Mexico inevitable. A monument to this incident is located in the Plaza directly across from the barracks, and the Bear Flag, despite its ignominious origin, is now the official flag of the State of California.

Also located in the Plaza, at #453 First Street East, is the 1913 Carnegie Public Library, presently housing the Chamber of Commerce. Its offices are open Monday through Friday, from 9:00 am to 5:00 pm, Saturday, 9:00 am to 4:00 pm, and Sunday, from 9:00 am to 3:00 pm. Here you can obtain additional information and maps of Sonoma.

As you circle the Plaza, it is hard to miss the Sebastiani Theater on the left, an impressive two-story pink structure with a 72-foot tower. Samuele Sebastiani is best known as the founder of the winery which bears his name, but he was also responsible for the construction of several significant buildings in Sonoma. The theater was one of his major projects and is a typical movie palace of the 1930's.

On the corner, at #498 First Street East, is an interesting brick commercial building. Constructed as the Duhring General Store in 1891, it features a short tower adorned by a flag pole. Also notice the row of commercial stone buildings to the left down East Napa, built of basalt from local quarries at about the same time.

Turn right on East Napa Street. As you reach Broadway (Highway 12), you will see the Mission Revival style City Hall, situated in the center of the Plaza. Built between 1906 and 1908 of stone from local quarries, all four sides are identical, so merchants on each side of the Plaza would be satisfied that the building "faced" their direction.

City Hall

Pause here for a look down Broadway, once the grand boulevard entrance into Sonoma. This spot also marks the end of El Camino Real, "the King's Highway," the road connecting all the missions. On the corner, at #500 Broadway, is the Old Bank Building, erected in 1875. Orginally it had two stories, but the second story collapsed in the 1906 earthquake. It still houses a bank.

Go right at the next intersection to view the buildings along First Street West. The two-story Leese-Fitch Adobe, at #485-495, was built about 1836 and was successively owned by two of General Vallejo's brothers-in-law. The next group of buildings dates from the 1860's to the early 1900's and presents a variety of interesting architectural styles.

At the far end of the block is the Salvador Vallejo Adobe at #415-427. Constructed in the early 1840's by Indian laborers for the General's brother, it was originally one story. The portion closest to the corner was destroyed in the 1906 earthquake and has been rebuilt, but the other section is authentic.

Across Spain Street from the adobe is the Sonoma Hotel. When built in the 1870's, stores and saloons occupied the lower floor, and there was a social hall on the second. Converted to a hotel in the 1920's, it still offers travelers a place to stay the night.

Turn right on Spain Street. The three-story Sebastiani apartment building, from 1938, contains the first elevator installed in Sonoma. Next door, at #18, is the Swiss Hotel, a Monterey Colonial style adobe home built in 1840 by Salvador Vallejo and his wife, the sister of Mrs. General Vallejo. It became a hotel in the 1880's and is now a restaurant.

The open space next to the Sonoma Cheese Factory was the site of La Casa Grande, the home completed in 1840 for General Vallejo, his wife Francisca Benicia, and their family. Eleven of their 16 children were born there. This imposing dwelling overlooked the Plaza and featured a three-story tower from which the General could survey the countryside. La Casa Grande was one of the largest and best furnished private residences in California and attracted visitors from all over the world. In 1867, after the family had moved to their new home, Lachryma Montis, the house burned, leaving only the adobe Indian servants' quarters.

Next you will come to the Toscano Hotel, at #20 East Spain Street. Originally built as a general store in the mid 1850's, it became a hotel in 1877. It has been appointed with turn-of-the-century furniture by the Sonoma League for Historic Preservation, which offers free tours on weekends from 1:00 to 4:00 pm and on Mondays from 11:00 am to 1:00 pm. The lobby is open for viewing daily from 10:00 am to 5:00 pm. The wooden structure in the rear was built in 1902 as a kitchen and dining hall for the hotel. (Restrooms are located behind the dining hall.)

This completes your tour of the Plaza. To leave the center of Sonoma, again ride south on First Street East, going past East Napa. Ahead you will see the striking white First Baptist Church. Known as Ames Chapel when built in the 1850's, this Gothic Revival house of worship was one of the first Protestant churches north of San Francisco. The steeple was added in 1868 by the Methodist Church which owned it at the time.

Further down the the street, at #564, is a unique Carpenter Gothic cottage with intricate trim, the only one of its type in Sonoma. It dates from the late 1850's.

Across the street is the Nash-Patton Adobe at #579. It was built in 1847 for John Nash, first American to be alcalde (mayor) in Sonoma under Mexican rule. Nash was arrested here by Lt. William Tecumseh

Sherman when he refused to turn over his office to the mayor appointed by the American government after annexation. This house, typifying small adobes of the period, has been carefully restored.

Go left at the corner onto Patten Street and left again at Second Street East. At the other end of the block you will see two of the finest houses in Sonoma. On the right, at #532, is the Duhring House, a large two-story Colonial Revival mansion built about 1859 for a leading family of the community. Frederick and Dorothea had humble beginnings, though, arriving from Germany without a penny. They sold Mrs. Duhring's trousseau and used the money to start a small business which eventually brought them prosperity.

Across the street, at #531, is the elegant Clewe House, a fine example of Italianate architecture in a picturesque setting. It was built in 1876 for cousins of Mrs. Duhring.

Turn around and ride south on Second Street East, going right when it dead-ends at MacArthur Street. Cross Broadway, and continue to Fifth Street West, turning left. At Leveroni Road, make a right turn, crossing over the creek. When the road ends at Arnold Drive, go left.

In a short distance, on the right, is the entrance to Temelec Adult Community. Turn in on Almeria Drive, taking the first right onto Temelec Circle and continuing about half a mile until you see a stone carriage house on your right and a magnificent stone mansion on your left. Go around the center divider to see **Temelec Hall**, one of the state's most impressive 19th century homes, now a private country club.

This three-story mansion complete with cupola was built in 1858 by Captain Granville Perry Swift of the Bear Flag Party for his bride. He wanted a home which was grander than General Vallejo's Lachryma Montis, and he succeeded. It is said that Swift kept Indian laborers virtually as slaves to construct this house of locally quarried basalt rock. The house may have cost as much as $250,000, money Swift made from gold mining. Swift's good fortune did not last, however. His wife divorced him, financial reverses beset him, and he was killed when his mule threw him over an embankment.

After admiring this stately building, return along Temelec and Almeria to Arnold Drive. Watch for traffic as you turn left.

If you are doing one of the shorter rides, go back the way you came, turning right on Leveroni and left onto Fifth Street West, just past the bridge, as you head toward General Vallejo's home to compare it with Swift's. Continue on Fifth, past MacArthur, all the way into town, crossing Highway 12 (which now follows Napa Street). In about 4 blocks, just past Claudia, turn right onto the paved bike path.

Optional side trip: *To ride the 16.5 mile side trip to Glen Ellen, do not turn onto Leveroni Road, but instead continue on Arnold Drive. The road is mostly flat and will have stretches of good surface with a shoulder, alternating with rough, narrow pavement and no shoulder. Traffic may also be heavy. Still, it is a much better route than the alternative Highway 12, where traffic moves at freeway speeds and bicyclists have little or no shoulder at all.*

The 7 mile route to Glen Ellen will take you past vineyards, old farms and new homes. Before you reach the town, you will pass the pleasant grounds of Sonoma Developmental Center. Established in 1891, it was the first hospital west of the Mississippi for the care of the mentally retarded. From here you will have one last mile of narrow rough road before reaching Glen Ellen.

Glen Ellen is a quaint little town that had its start when General Vallejo built a sawmill along Sonoma Creek in the 1840's. Frenchman Joshua Chavet settled here in 1856 and established vineyards and a winery, attracting other vintners. The town was named in 1869, after the wife of a pioneer winegrower, and the post office established two years later.

The town's boom period occurred when the railroad reached Glen Ellen in 1879, bringing large groups of tourists to camp or stay in cottages and hotels. By the turn of the century the tiny town had become a boisterous place with numerous hotels, saloons and brothels.

Jack London came to Glen Ellen on vacation in 1903, shortly after publication of his first major novel, Call of the Wild. Here he met Charmian Kitteridge whom he married in 1905 after divorcing his first wife. He and Charmian made Glen Ellen their home for the rest of their lives.

Jack London, one of California's most widely read and prolific authors, was born in San Francisco in 1876 and grew up in Oakland. He escaped the poverty of his youth by world-wide travel and adventure, including gold mining in the Alaskan Klondike. He was a ruggedly handsome, hard-working, hard-drinking man of socialist ideals with a love of books and a passion for writing. He sold his first story at the age of 22 and was America's highest paid author by the time he was 30. In his short lifetime (he died of uremic poisoning at the age of 40) he wrote 51 books, nearly 200 short stories and numerous articles.

Jack London State Historic Park is located on a wooded hillside outside of Glen Ellen and includes London's ranch, the museum House of Happy Walls, and the ruins of Wolf House. To reach the park, take London Ranch Road, just past the country store. (This is a good place to buy supplies if you plan to picnic in the park.) The 1.3 mile climb to the park is moderately strenuous, the first part being the steepest.

On the way, you will pass the entrance to Glen Ellen Winery, located on one of Sonoma Valley's historic wine estates. On the property is a house built by the pioneer Wegner family in the 1860's, as well as other old buildings. The tasting room is open daily from 10:00 am to 5:00 pm.

At the end of London Ranch Road is the entrance to the park, free to bicyclists. You will want to allow one to two hours to see everything and perhaps enjoy a picnic lunch.

A right turn just inside the entrance, toward the overflow parking lot, will take you to the Londons' beloved Beauty Ranch, where Jack practiced scientific agriculture and entertained his many friends. Here is the small cottage dating from 1862 where he lived, wrote and died. Here also are stone barns, concrete silos and the "Pig Palace," a luxurious circular building he designed for his hogs, all located on a half mile walk.

To the left of the park entrance, through the parking lot, is the path to the House of Happy Walls, the house Charmian London built in 1919 as a memorial to her husband. She lived alone in this large stone dwelling until her death in 1955 at the age of 84. Today the building houses a museum and includes the South Sea collection gathered on the couple's two year sailing voyage in 1907-09, as well as other London memorabilia. The museum is open daily, 10:00 am to 5:00 pm. (Restrooms can be found near the parking lot.)

Wolf House

From the museum, be sure to take the half mile trail down through the trees to the ruins of fated Wolf House. The Londons began building it in 1911, using native volcanic lava boulders and redwood timbers. It contained 26 rooms, 9 fireplaces, and a courtyard reflection pool. Late one night in 1913, just a few weeks before the Londons planned to move in, this magnificent house was mysteriously destroyed by fire. It was never rebuilt. All that is left are the stone walls and chimneys, an eerie monument to the author's dream.

Three years later Jack London suddenly died. As he wished, his ashes are buried on a wooded knoll off the trail to Wolf House near the graves of two pioneer children. The site is marked by a huge lava boulder, too large for use in Wolf House. Charmian's ashes are here also.

When you have finished your exploration of this beautiful and romantic park, return to Glen Ellen, enjoying the thrilling downhill run. Go right on Arnold Drive, heading back toward Sonoma.

Ride on Arnold Drive for approximately 5 miles until you reach Verano Street, just opposite the small white steepled church, where you turn left. Continue on Verano across Highway 12 to its end at Fifth Street West. Follow the road to the right, and in about 3 blocks, just past Linda Drive, take a left onto the paved bike path. You have now rejoined the main route of the ride.

Main route continues: Once on the bike path, you will see the buildings of Lachryma Montis to your left across the open field. Turn left when you come to the narrow road lined with cottonwood trees which leads to the **Vallejo Home**.

In 1851 General Vallejo built this fine two-story Victorian Gothic Revival residence, with its twin porches, dormer windows, elaborately carved wooden trim, and a marble fireplace in each room. Prefabricated in the East, the house was shipped around the Horn. Vallejo named his estate Lachryma Montis ("mountain tear") for the free-flowing spring on the property. Grapevines, fruit trees, decorative trees and shrubs covered the land. A special brick warehouse, used to store wine, fruit and other produce, is today known as the Swiss Chalet and serves as a museum for the Vallejo Home, part of the State Historic Park.

Mariano Guadalupe Vallejo was born in Monterey, California, in 1807. When he was 16, he became a military cadet in the Monterey Company. He rose rapidly through the ranks and was named Commander of the Presidio of San Francisco in 1831.

In 1834 Governor Jose Figueroa sent Vallejo north as Military Commander and Director of Colonization of the Northern Frontier with specific orders to take charge of the secularization of the mission at

Sonoma. This involved reducing it to the status of a parish church, freeing the Indian workers, and distributing the mission lands and other assets to the general population.

As a reward, Vallejo was granted Rancho Petaluma, 44,000 acres of prime agricultural land. With additional acquisitions, Vallejo eventually owned 175,000 acres. This vast empire, together with his extensive military and civil powers, made Vallejo one of the wealthiest and most influential men in California. He was in total charge of the area north of San Francisco Bay while California was a Mexican province. He surveyed and established the Pueblo of Sonoma, gave land grants to private citizens, and directed military affairs.

His circumstances suddenly changed with the Bear Flag Revolt. Freed after his imprisonment and allowed to return home, Vallejo found that his rancho had been stripped of its horses, cattle and other commodities by the Bear Flaggers. Vallejo's vast political and economic power had evaporated.

Vallejo continued to play a part in government for a number of years. He was a delegate to California's constitutional convention in 1848 and was elected to the State Senate in 1850. After he was unsuccessful in his plans to establish a state capital at what is now the town of Vallejo, he limited his political activities to the local level, serving two terms as mayor of Sonoma.

Vallejo Home Cookhouse

General Vallejo and his wife lived here at Lachryma Montis for over 35 years. Gradually, it became necessary to sell nearly all their vast land holdings, as the General suffered one economic setback after another. During his last years, he lived quietly, spending his time reading and writing letters to his many children and friends. He also authored a five volume history of California and was an active supporter of the California Horticultural Society. He died in 1890 at the age of 82 and was buried in the nearby Sonoma Mountain Cemetery.

In addition to the house and museum, the park contains several other interesting smaller buildings to investigate. There are also picnic tables under the trees by the pool and restrooms near the entrance. When you are ready to leave the last home of this important native Californian, ride back out to the bike path and continue on your way.

As you cross First Street West notice the Depot Hotel on the left. Built in 1870 of stone from General Vallejo's quarries, it was originally a home with walls 16" thick. It was bought by the railroad in 1888 to be used as a saloon for travelers. Today it is a restaurant.

Continue on the bike path to the park where the **Sonoma Valley Railroad Depot** is located. This replica of the original 1880 building houses the Sonoma Valley Historical Society museum, open from 1:00 to 4:30 pm, Wednesday through Sunday. The bike path on which you are riding is actually the old railroad right of way.

In a block and a half, at #315 Second Street East on the right, is the Vella Cheese Company. It is housed in the 1905 Sonoma Brewing Company Building. Vella, along with the Sonoma Cheese Factory on the Plaza, makes Monterey Jack, the only type of cheese native to the West.

As you approach the end of the bike path on Fourth Street East, you will ride through historic vineyards belonging to the Sebastiani Winery. The buildings are located to the right on Fourth Street East.

Samuele Sebastiani came to California from Italy and worked the stone quarries on Schocken Hill. By 1904 he had saved enough money to buy both an old winery and these vineyards, first planted by the mission padres in 1825 and later owned by Vallejo.

Sebastiani's son and grandson have followed in his footsteps, producing both bulk and premium wines. The tasting room is open from 10:00 am to 5:00 pm daily, and tours are offered throughout the day. There is also an interesting Indian Artifacts Museum.

From here you may either return to the Plaza or continue to another historic winery. The route to Buena Vista is not recommended for inexperienced riders, however. Although the road is flat and scenic, and adds only 3.5 miles, the last very narrow section may be difficult to navigate if there is much traffic. If you are returning to your starting point from Sebastiani's, proceed down Fourth Street, turning right at the corner onto East Spain Street.

Optional extension: *To continue to Buena Vista Winery, ride in the other direction on Fourth Street. Turn right onto Lovall Valley Road, opposite the bike path. When the road seems to end, go left, then right, staying to the right, as you follow the signs to Buena Vista. When you reach Old Winery Road, turn left and follow the narrow, eucalyptus lined driveway to its end at the winery.*

    Buena Vista Winery*, one of California's oldest, was founded in 1857 by Hungarian Count Agoston Haraszthy. In this tranquil setting, he raised massive stone buildings and had cellars dug into limestone hillsides, eventually making Buena Vista one of the leading wine producers in the state. The count also was responsible for importing hundreds of European grape varieties, which were distributed throughout the area. He came to an untimely end on a trip to Nicaragua in 1869, disappearing in the jungle, some say eaten by alligators.*

    The winery remained in operation, run by two sons (married to two of Vallejo's daughters) until the earthquake of 1906. It was reopened and the buildings restored in the 1940's. Today the actual wine-making is done elsewhere, but you can take a self-guided tour of the cellars and enjoy the tasting room, originally the press house. It is open from 10:00 am to 5:00 pm daily. There are also shady picnic facilities and restrooms on the grounds.

    Leaving pleasant Buena Vista, stay on Old Winery Road until it terminates at East Napa Street. Go right, heading back toward central Sonoma. At Fourth Street East turn right and then left in one block onto East Spain Street.

Main route continues: In a short distance on East Spain, you will come upon two more old houses of note. #245, on the left, is one of the earliest wood frame houses built in Sonoma. The oldest portion dates from the 1850's. On the corner, at #205, is an adobe with a two-story veranda. The wooden back section was built in 1846 and the front adobe part added in 1851, after the owner struck it rich in the gold fields. The adobe walls are 22 inches thick.

Notice also the small single-story stone house in the next block, at #147, just before the Blue Wing Inn. A stone worker built it with rubble from the quarry on Schocken Hill, to your right, where he worked. It dates from 1906.

The Schocken Quarry was only one of the many granite and basalt quarries in the Sonoma area, but it was among the largest. In the

1880's and '90's, quarries were Sonoma's third most important industry, after wineries and dairies. The quarries furnished paving blocks for the streets of San Francisco, Petaluma and San Jose until the use of asphalt destroyed the business.

The two-story Blue Wing Inn dates from about 1840. This Monterey Colonial style adobe was probably built to house soldiers and travelers. In 1849 it became the Sonoma House, a hotel, saloon, and stage depot. Still looking very much as it did then, today it contains antique shops.

When you reach the mission, turn right and then left into the parking lot to find your car. This concludes your ride through Sonoma, one of the most historic and interesting towns in the state.

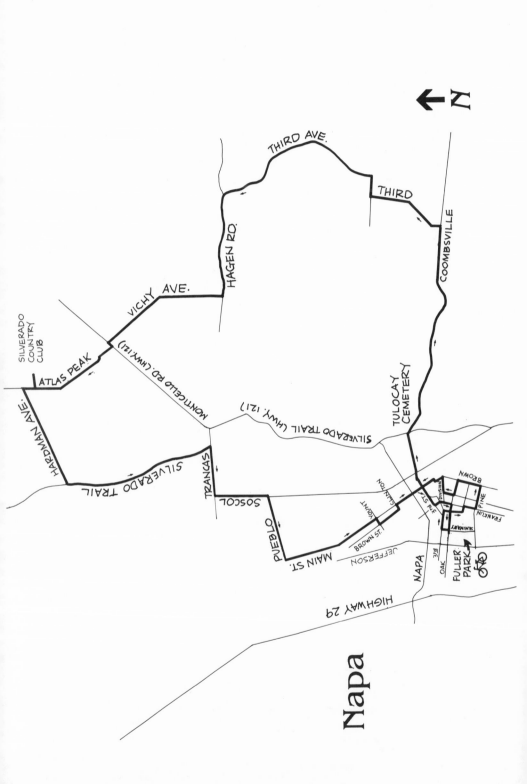

Napa

Napa

Distance: 16 miles

Rating: Although rated **moderate** because of the rolling hills outside of the city of Napa, much of this ride is flat. The country roads are mostly unshaded and thus may be hot in the summer. This tour is especially pleasant in the fall when vineyards turn red and gold and grapes are being harvested.

Highlights: Napa was once a major river port and center of the Napa Valley wine country. This ride offers a glimpse of the city's glorious past, with many outstanding examples of 19th century commercial and residential architecture. The route into the countryside takes you by acres of vineyards and to an historic winery.

Skirted by highways leading into the Napa Valley, the city of Napa is often passed by unnoticed. But a century ago, when the Napa River served as a main transportation route to the valley, it was a bustling port. As such, it played a valuable part in the development of the local wine industry. Eventually river transportation was replaced by truck, and the city's importance faded. Now, after a prolonged lull, Napa is gradually becoming a center of activity once again, as visitors discover its many charms.

The word "Napa" was probably derived from the Nappa tribe of Indians who lived in this area for centuries. When pioneer George Yount arrived here in 1831, he estimated that the Indian population in the Napa Valley numbered between 10,000 and 12,000. But, as happened in other areas, the Indians did not survive the invasion of the white settlers. Thousands died during a cholera epidemic in 1833 and within a decade the native population was decimated.

The original town site of Napa was surveyed in 1848 by Nathan Coombs, and the first building, a saloon, was erected a year later. Napa, with its drinking establishments, theater, reading room, band, and other amenities, became a favorite place for gold miners to escape the worst of the winter weather.

European grape cuttings were planted south of town in 1852, and Charles Krug produced the first European style wine in the Napa region in 1858. The wine industry flourished at least in part because of the city's location on the navigational head of the Napa River. Schooners plied her waters in the 1840's, and a steamship line to San Francisco was established in 1850, providing inexpensive and reliable transportation to the metropolitan market place. The city of Napa controlled the region's trade for almost a century until the advent of the motor trucking system brought an end to the river's usefulness. Now it is used mainly for recreation.

Begin your ride of Napa at Fuller Park, located at the intersection of Jefferson and Oak Streets, a few blocks from First Street. (Restrooms are available in the park.) The surrounding neighborhood is well known for its many fine examples of 19th century architecture, ranging from small cottages to splendid mansions.

From the park, ride on Oak Street, away from Jefferson, where you will see the first of the charming homes in this area. Turning left at Seminary, admire the beautifully restored Eastlake style house on the corner, at #705. At the other end of the block is #741, one of the most elaborate homes you will see on this tour, with a profusion of spindles, turned columns and brackets. This 1892 Queen Anne was designed by popular local architect Luther Turton for the family of William Andrews, a grocer.

Napa Victorian

A right turn brings you onto busy Third Street. In one block, note the houses on the corners, #1561 and #1562, built in the simpler Italianate style and dating from the late 1870's. After another block, stay to the right as the street divides. There, at #1475 Fourth Street, on the corner of Even Street, is the fanciful **Migliavacca Mansion** with its three-story tower. Also designed by Luther Turton, this residence was built in 1895 for Giuseppe Migliavacca and his family of ten children for a cost of only $4000. Migliavacca was in the wine business and associated with the Bank of Italy, forerunner of the Bank of America. Originally located several blocks away, the house was moved to this site to make room for a new library.

Ride down narrow Even Street, continuing to its end. At Laurel Street, go left for one block and then right on Franklin Street. This tree-lined avenue is one of the prettiest in town. On one end of the block, at #397, is the late 1870's Italianate double house, built for the founder of Sawyer Tanning and Woolen Mill. At the other end, at #313, is the Holden Mansion, dating from 1886. Samuel Holden served as president of the Sawyer Mill, as well as a bank director, city council member, and college president. Most of the workers in the mill were Chinese who lived in a thriving Chinatown located on Main Street.

A left turn takes you onto Pine, and in 3 blocks, you will go left again at Brown Street. In the next block are two of Napa's most impressive old residences. #443 Brown was built about 1889 for Edward Manasse, the developer of a new process for tanning glove leather and a partner with Holden in the tanning mill. Beyond, at #485, is the fine home built about the same time for Edward S. Churchill, a banker and vintner. The porch and columns were added later. This elegant structure, now a bed and breakfast inn, is on the National Register of Historic Places.

Go left on Oak Street where, on the right, at #1120, you will see a three-story home with a mansard roof. When it was built in 1872 for George Goodman, Sr., it faced Brown Street. Now apartments fill its front yard and have blocked its view. Goodman had a general store and started the first bank in Napa.

At the next corner, to the left, is a large brown shingle home at #486 Coombs. Located directly behind the Churchill mansion, it was built in 1893 by Edward S. Churchill for his son, Edward W. Later it became the Cedar Gables Inn, a boarding house, but has now been restored as a private residence.

In another block, at #492 Randolph Street, is the house built in the 1880's by George Goodman, Sr., for his son George, Jr. It is a typical Queen Anne style with corner tower and elaborate entrance porch.

Manasse House

From this corner you can also see further down the block the 1920's home at #447. Its most famous resident was actress Carole Lombard, who stayed here in the 1940's when she and Charles Laughton were in Napa to film the movie *They Knew What They Wanted.*

Going right on Randolph Street, you will find more fascinating period homes, especially #569 on the corner with its white wrought iron fence. It was constructed in 1879. At Division Street, turn right and stop a moment to see three buildings at this intersection designed by Luther Turton. The Methodist Church dates from 1916. Across the street from the church, at #608 Randolph, is a large Queen Anne with a corner tower from about 1890. At the corner where two streets merge is a blue shingle style home constructed about the same time. Of special interest is the way the second story shingles are "draped" about the side windows. The simpler shingle style house was developed in reaction to the profuse ornamentation of Victorian structures and flourished longer in California than in any other part of the country.

The Gothic Revival style predates the Victorian Era, and a charming example can be found next door at #1236 Division, a small cottage dating from 1860. Contrast this with the lovely Queen Anne across the street at #1225. This home was built around 1882 by George Goodman, Sr., for his son Harvey. It is now a bed and breakfast inn.

At the end of the block, at #1211, is a large Eastlake home built in 1887 for Theodore Parker, superintendent of the early Napa Gas Works, at a cost of $5000. Currently, it houses law offices.

Continue along Division past the City/County Library (formerly the location of Migliavacca's mansion and winery), going left on Brown and right on Fifth Street. From here you can see the brick Hatt Building, originally a grain mill, dating from 1884. Follow the road left onto Main Street. Bordering the river, Main Street was once the center of Napa, but as water transportation became less important, commercial growth occurred away from the river. Now the downtown plan calls for redevelopment of this historic waterfront area.

When you reach Third Street, just before Veterans Memorial Park, turn right, going over the Napa River on the narrow bridge. After crossing Silverado Trail (Highway 121), angle to the right on Coombsville Road, named for Nathan Coombs, the founder of Napa. You will have a bike lane here and a gradual uphill.

Tulocay Cemetery, on the left, is the final resting place of many of Napa's citizens, including Mammy Pleasant, infamous madam and voodoo queen, and Cayetano Juarez, owner of Rancho Tulocay. Juarez donated part of his land grant for this cemetery in 1859. Although records only go back to 1873, undoubtedly earlier burials took place. Bicycles are not allowed in the cemetery, so if you wish to explore, you will have to do so on foot.

As you continue on Coombsville Road, you will soon be out into the countryside and away from the congestion of the city. Your views will be of open fields and the hills beyond. When you reach Third Avenue in about 1.5 miles, go left. In less than a mile, Third turns right and the road narrows, but traffic is light. You will ride by acres of vineyards, along a tree-lined ravine, and past the Napa Valley Country Club. After 2.5 miles, the road goes left and becomes Hagen Road. In a short distance is the Welcome Grange, officially known as the Mt. George Farm Center, built in 1916 with volunteer labor, money and materials. Grange meetings are still held here regularly.

Make the next right turn onto Vichy Avenue. You will ride on rolling hills for just over a mile until Vichy ends at Monticello Road (Highway 121). Go left, then take the first right onto Atlas Peak Road.

Before long, you will come to the Quail Ridge Wine Cellars. This was originally the Hedgeside Winery, constructed of native stone in 1885 for Morris Estee, national leader of the GOP and 1882 candidate for governor. The architect was Hamden McIntrye, who also designed Inglenook Winery and Christian Brothers Greystone Cellars in Napa Valley. There are 450 feet of tunnels, hand dug into the hillside by Chinese laborers, and still used today for aging wine. The house next door was originally part of the winery but has since been converted to a private residence.

The entrance to the Silverado Country Club is just over half a mile further along. The country club is located on what was once the 1200 acre estate of Civil War General John Miller, and the club house is in his 1870 mansion.

After viewing General Miller's home, return to Atlas Peak, going right. Make the first left at Hardman Avenue, and when you reach the Silverado Trail, turn left. Here you will have a wide shoulder as you pass still more vineyards and farms. In about 1.5 miles, the road ends at Trancas Street, where you go right, back toward Napa. Turn left at the traffic light onto Soscol Avenue.

To leave this congested street, go right at Pueblo in half a mile. In another half mile, before reaching busy Jefferson Street, turn left on Main Street. Less than a mile further along, just before Yount Street, at #1727 Main, is a Queen Anne Victorian home built in 1889 for Dr. Hennessey. A right turn on Yount brings you to another historic winery.

In 1882 Joseph Mathews, a native of Portugal, built the Lisbon Winery. He pioneered exportation of fine Napa wines to Europe and developed a prize-winning sherry. Structures that remain from that time include the sandstone building where wine was made and a brick one for sherry-making. Before prohibition, there were several other wineries along the river front, but this is the only such facility left in the city.

From Yount, turn left onto Brown, and ride until the road ends at Clinton, where you go left back to Main Street. Here, on the corner, is the old Pfeiffer Building, now the Andrews Meat Co. & Deli. Constructed in 1875 as a brewery, this two-story sandstone building later was a saloon (and possibly a brothel) and, for 50 years, a Chinese laundry. It is the oldest surviving commercial structure in Napa.

Go right on Main Street to see more of downtown Napa's historic buildings. The Napa Opera House, at #1018 Main, dates from about 1879. Originally, it served as the social center of the community, but with the decline of traveling shows and the increased popularity of movies, the Opera House was closed in 1914. It is now being restored for use by a small theater company.

Architect Luther Turton designed commercial buildings as well as residences, and examples of his work can be found at the corner of First Street. The Winship Building, at #948 Main, has a carved wooden cornice and jutting bay window. Commissioned in 1888 by a doctor for his second-floor practice and street-level stores, it now houses offices and speciality shops. Next to it, at #975 First Street, is the elegant Semorile Building, also dating from 1888. It was constructed for an Italian grocer and is distinguished by the unusual combination of brick, stone, and wrought iron on its façade.

Winship Building

Additional commercial buildings from the early part of the century can be found on First Streeet on the other side of Main, although traffic there is generally too heavy for pleasant bicycling. Of special note is the 1901 Goodman Library, at #1219 First, designed by Turton and constructed of native stone in the Richardsonian Romanesque style. Built with funds donated by George Goodman, Sr., and used as a library until 1963, it is now the home of the Napa County Historical Society.

In the next block on the corner is a beautiful Classical Revival bank building, dating from 1923. Be sure to note its fine interior. An interesting contrast is the Art Deco building across the street, once the home of the Oberon Bar. Constructed of wood in the 1880's, the saloon was rebuilt with its present glazed tile façade after a devastating fire in the early 1930's. Today it houses a restaurant and shops.

Make a right turn at Third Street, and in another block you will find the Napa County Court House. When completed in 1879, it had an onion-shaped bell tower, but this was removed in the 1930's. Next you will see the First Presbyterian Church built in 1879 in the Victorian Gothic style. This wooden structure is well preserved inside and out and is now a California Registered Historical Landmark.

Passing the church, continue on Third one block, going left at Franklin. From Franklin, make a right turn at Oak, which brings you back to Fuller Park and the end of your ride. You will have experienced the many delights of this historic port city that once played such an important role in the growth of the Napa Valley wine industry.

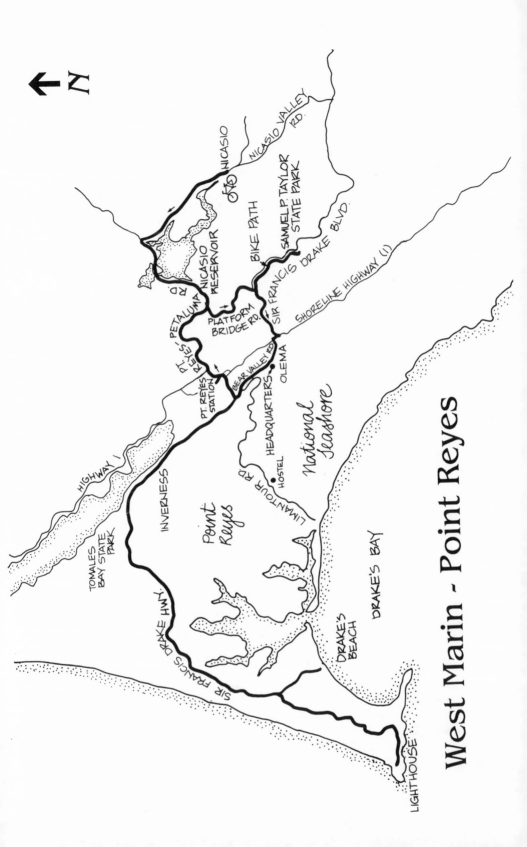

West Marin ~ Point Reyes

West Marin - Point Reyes

Distance: 30 miles with optional side trips of 30 or 38 miles

Rating: The main route is rated **moderate**. It travels on country roads through small towns and along a bike path in the state park. It is generally rolling except for one short steep hill near Olema and some gradual uphill. The longer rides are **strenuous** and include lots of climbing. There is no shoulder much of the way and traffic may be heavy, especially near the National Seashore Headquarters, but the roads are wide enough to accommodate both cars and cyclists.

Highlights: On this tour you can enjoy the peacefulness of open countryside and wooded glens as you visit interesting old western towns, the multifaceted Point Reyes National Seashore, and the site of an historic paper mill in Samuel P. Taylor State Park. The optional routes take you to the Point Reyes peninsula, to either Drake's Beach or the lighthouse, and offer views of the ocean and the bay where Sir Francis Drake may have landed in 1579.

Begin your ride in the tiny village of Nicasio, located on Nicasio Valley Road off Sir Francis Drake Boulevard, less than an hour north of San Francisco. (The turnoff is at the San Geronimo Golf Club.)

Nicasio began as part of one of Marin County's most extensive land grants, Rancho Nicasio, and was once much larger than it is today. For many years the town was a thriving center for the local cattle and dairy ranches. It had numerous businesses and stores, including a racetrack and large three-story hotel whose guests arrived by stagecoach.

By 1863 Nicasio hoped to become the Marin county seat, and the large open square was laid out in the center of town as a site for the courthouse. The town lost its bid to San Rafael, however, and now the area is used for baseball games and town barbecues.

The most significant turning point in Nicasio's history occurred in 1875 when the railroads came to Marin, but not to Nicasio. From that time on, the town's size and importance dwindled. Today, only a few buildings and homes are left. Of special interest is the small steepled Old St. Mary's Catholic Church on one side of the square. It dates from 1867. (No food or restrooms are available in town.)

Nicasio Schoolhouse

Leave Nicasio by heading north on Nicasio Valley Road. On the outskirts of town is its most famous landmark, the red Nicasio schoolhouse built in 1871. It served as a school as late as 1949 but is now a private residence

The open road here is pleasant riding with views of the Nicasio Reservoir and the grassy hills of the West Marin countryside. In 3.4 miles when the road ends, go left onto Point Reyes-Petaluma Road. Now you will have 3 miles of gentle downhill. At the stop sign, Point Reyes-Pelatuma Road turns right over a bridge, but you keep going straight ahead onto Platform Bridge Road. This secluded wooded road is narrow but lightly traveled. It parallels Lagunitas Creek, also known as Paper Mill Creek.

In a little more than 2 miles the road ends at Sir Francis Drake Boulevard. Just before you reach the stop sign, turn right on a gravel road which takes you over the creek on the arched 1933 Platform Bridge. On the other side of the bridge, to your left, is the beginning of the bike path to **Samuel P. Taylor State Park**. It is marked as the "Cross Marin Trail."

The bike path continues along Paper Mill Creek and takes you into a cool forest of second growth redwoods, a marked change from the open hills you have just left. At the end of the 2 mile bike path, go around the gate. (Restrooms can be found here.) Ride on the service road a very short distance to the site of Samuel Taylor's paper mill. Built in 1856, it was the first on the Pacific coast. The mill was originally powered by water and later by steam. It produced newsprint, bags, election ballots, and other paper supplies for San Francisco.

A small town called Taylorville grew up around the mill. In the 1870's the North Pacific Coast Railroad came through, bringing sightseers to the mill pond and the shady forests. A campground and three-story hotel were built, and the area became a popular weekend resort. The mill went out of business during the depression of 1893, and the buildings burned in 1915.

Past the mill site are campgrounds, including one for bicyclists, restrooms with hot showers, a swimming hole, picnic grounds, and hiking trails. Call the park at 415-488-9897 for information.

Return along the bike path, making a sharp left at its end to reach Sir Francis Drake Highway. Here you may encounter fast-moving traffic, so exercise caution. Turn right and pedal up the hill. This is a fairly strenuous climb over Bolinas Ridge but is only about half a mile long. You are rewarded by a fast run into the little town of Olema, located at the intersection with Highway 1.

Olema, founded in 1859, once bustled with activity. It was one of Marin's most important early towns, but, like Nicasio, its importance began to fade when the railroad bypassed it in 1875, going instead through Point Reyes Station.

The town's centerpiece is the old Nelson Hotel, dating from 1876. Restored as the Olema Inn, it provides bed and board for guests. This attractive building is of Shaker design, probably the only one of its kind in California. A short distance south on Highway 1 is a private home which was once the meeting hall of the United Ancient Order of Druids, a fraternal organization. It dates from 1881.

Food is available in Olema at the store or restaurant. Note that if you plan to do the longer rides, you will need to purchase supplies either here or in Inverness.

From Sir Francis Drake Highway, turn right onto Highway 1. At the next corner, go left on Bear Valley Road. Ride to the **Point Reyes National Seashore Visitor Center**, a distance of half a mile. Nearly all of the triangular Point Reyes peninsula, over 65,000 acres, is part of this wild and spacious park.

Point Reyes has a fascinating geological history. It is separated from the rest of Marin County by the Olema Valley, which follows the San Andreas Fault from Bolinas Lagoon in the south to Tomales Bay in the north. It is estimated that this piece of land is moving northward about two inches per year, sliding ahead when an earthquake occurs.

For thousands of years before the Spanish arrived, this area was inhabited by the peaceful and spiritual Coast Miwok Indians. They lived in small communities of dome-shaped huts covered with tule rushes or redwood bark. Their diet consisted of shellfish, fresh water fish, venison, and bread made from acorn flour.

The establishment of Mission San Rafael brought an end to the Indians' way of life. They were relocated and nearly all died from smallpox and other European diseases, as well as from the psychological trauma of forced mission life.

Olema Inn

Once a land grant known as Rancho Punta de los Reyes Sobrante, Point Reyes became the first great dairy center of California after the United States annexed it in 1846. You can see remnants of this period in the few remaining ranches, including the old Bear Valley Ranch, where park headquarters is now located.

The Visitor Center, open weekdays from 9:00 am to 5:00 pm and weekends from 8:00 am to 5:00 pm, has exhibits and information about the park and its facilities. There is also a seismograph for monitoring earthquake activity, as well as restrooms and picnic tables. Nearby is the self-guided Earthquake Trail, a hike of less than a mile which follows the San Andreas Fault, close to the epicenter of the 1906 earthquake. You will also find it worthwhile to take the short walk to Kule Loklo, an authentic replica of a Miwok village, including huts, sweathouse and dance house. The Visitor Center can be reached at 415-663-1092.

Go left as you leave the Visitor Center, and continue on Bear Valley Road. In a little over a mile, you will pass Limantour Road, the way to the Point Reyes Hostel, located in an old ranch house. The 6 mile route to the hostel is very strenuous. If you would like to spend the night, call 415-669-7414 for information.

Soon Bear Valley Road ends at Sir Francis Drake Highway. To do either of the optional routes, go left towards Inverness. To continue the easier main route, turn right on Drake Highway toward Point Reyes Station.

Optional side trips: *In planning a tour of the Point Reyes peninsula, you may wish to consider the season. Summer is the foggiest, but the weather often clears by noon. Winter can bring storms, but the clear days in between may be warm and sunny. Wildflowers are most abundant in the spring, and early fall has the warmest temperatures. Thus, any time of year can be good, although there is always the possibility of a strong wind off the ocean.*

To do either of the optional routes (30 miles round trip to Drake's Beach or 38 miles round trip to the lighthouse), continue 3 miles on Sir Francis Drake Highway to Inverness. This is a charming little resort community founded in 1889 along Tomales Bay. Here you can stock up on food for the remainder of your ride, as well as admire the photogenic old general store from the 1890's (now a gift shop) and the interesting assortment of piers and boathouses along the bay.

About a mile past the town the flat road ends and the hills begin. The first one over Inverness Ridge is the steepest, but is not long. Sir Francis Drake Highway now becomes a narrow road with no shoulder that climbs up and down over the coastal hills and pasture land of Point Reyes National Seashore.

Traffic is generally light except on clear weekend days in January, when the gray whales are migrating south. Then, hundreds of cars create traffic jams heading to the lighthouse to view these gentle giants on their way from the arctic seas to the lagoons of Baja, California. Safe and peaceful riding is better achieved at other times.

Just after the crest of the hill past Inverness is Pierce Point Road which leads to Tomales Bay State Park, a ride of about a mile. There is camping here for bicyclists. The beaches along the bay are more sheltered and thus tend to be warmer than those on the ocean. For information call 415-669-1140.

In another 2 miles you will begin to have grand views of the Pacific Ocean on your right and the arms of Drake's Estero with Drake's Bay beyond to your left. In several more miles, you will come to the turnoff to Drake's Beach.

The road to Drake's Beach is less than 2 miles long, with a short downhill. Here you will find a visitor center, snack bar (open weekends only in the winter, daily during the summer) and restrooms. The beach here is sheltered from strong ocean winds by the white sea cliffs.

Drake's Bay is named for Sir Francis Drake, the English admiral who is famous for his circumnavigation of the world in 1577-80. In 1579, having lost four of his five ships in the dangerous waters of the Straits of Magellan, Drake was looking for a sheltered harbor in which to repair his one remaining ship, the Golden Hinde. He found a protected spot somewhere along the northern California coast, went ashore, and spent a month resting and making repairs. The actual location of his landing is highly controversial, although many historians believe it was here at Drake's Bay.

To reach the lighthouse, the longer of the two optional routes, ride past the turnoff to Drake's Beach and continue 5 more miles along Sir Francis Drake Highway. There are several cattle grates crossing the road, so use caution. Pedal up the last hill to the **Point Reyes Lighthouse,** built in 1870 on the rocky tip of the peninsula. This is one of the windiest and foggiest places on the coast and the location of numerous shipwrecks, but a fascinating place to visit when the weather is clear. Tours of the lighthouse, reached by walking down 300 steps, are given on weekends. Check with the ranger at the visitor center, 415-669-1534. Restrooms are also available.

Point Reyes Lighthouse

You may want to picnic here while enjoying the views of the beach or watching the waves crash against the rocks. Then it is time to return back along the same route with its last exciting downhill into Inverness. When you reach the junction with Bear Valley Road, follow Sir Frances Drake Highway left to Point Reyes Station, and you will have rejoined the main route of the ride.

Main route continues: In less than a mile from the Bear Valley Road intersection, turn left onto Highway 1 (Shoreline Highway) over Lagunitas Creek. Follow the highway into the town of **Point Reyes Station**.

Originally just a stop on the railroad in 1875, this site was called Olema Station, and was connected to the town of Olema by stagecoach. In 1883 the name was changed, and the townsite laid out by Dr. Galen Burdell, a dentist who is considered to be the founder of the community. Purchasers of his town lots were prevented from selling liquor by a clause in the deeds. This restriction was not intended to keep the town dry, but rather to allow Dr. Burdell to maintain a monopoly on the sale of alcoholic beverages at his hotel and saloon. When a store across the street rebelled and began offering alcohol for sale, Burdell sued but lost the case. His hotel is gone now, but the rival tavern remains, today operating as the Western Saloon. It is located on the corner of A and Second Streets.

A or Main Street is the site of the old railroad right of way, as the tracks went right through the center of town. The former depot is now the post office. The train stopped running in 1933, and Point Reyes Station has changed little since then. It retains a rural charm that captivates visitors and residents alike. Hungry bicyclists will appreciate the several restaurants and markets located here.

Follow Highway 1 as it turns right at the other end of town. Take the first left onto Mesa Street for one block to #505. This large structure with its twin corner towers was built in 1914 as the Foresters Hall, a meeting place for the fraternal organization, and is now being restored as an art gallery.

Return to Highway 1, going left up the hill out of town. On the other side of the hill, take a right onto Point Reyes-Petaluma Road. This road is moderately rolling with good shoulder. In about 3 miles, at the stop sign, turn left (Platform Bridge Road goes right) and continue past the Nicasio Reservoir to Nicasio Valley Road. A right turn and 3 miles of pleasant riding will return you to your starting point in Nicasio. Whatever route you may have chosen, you will have had a splendid day of riding and sightseeing in this fascinating section of Marin County.

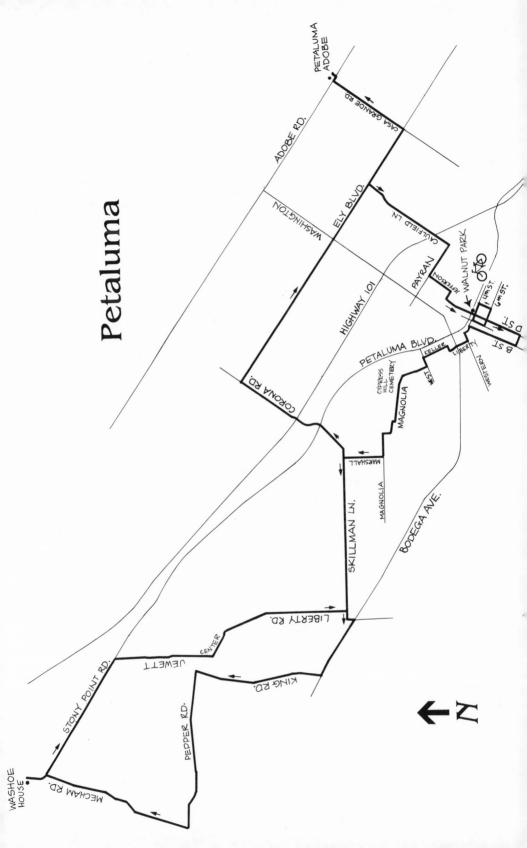

Petaluma

Petaluma

Distance: 15 miles with 15 mile optional side trip

Rating: With rolling hills, some narrow roads, and the possibility of city traffic, the shorter ride is rated **moderate**. The optional side trip adds more hills and is considered **moderately strenuous**. The roads outside of Petaluma are mostly unshaded and may be hot on a summer day.

Highlights: Undamaged by the 1906 earthquake, Petaluma has many fine Victorian homes and the West Coast's best collection of ironfront commercial buildings. You will also visit Petaluma Adobe State Historic Park, the rancho home of General Vallejo. The optional route takes you into the surrounding countryside, with its grassy hills and dairy farms, and to one of California's oldest roadhouses.

The Petaluma tribe of the Coast Miwok Indians were the first inhabitants of this area, enjoying the abundant wildlife along the river. The Petaluma River also brought the first Spanish explorers in 1776, followed in later years by soldiers who moved the Indians to missions established in San Francisco, San Rafael and nearby Sonoma. After the Mexican government ended the mission system in 1836, the land was divided into ranchos, the largest being Rancho Petaluma to the east of the river, granted to General Vallejo of Sonoma.

The history of the town itself began in 1850, the year California achieved statehood, with a hunters' camp along the river. Soon a village was well underway. In 1852 Garrett Keller laid out a town and sold lots, despite the fact they were part of a land grant he did not own. Petaluma quickly grew into a thriving port, its river providing a vital link between San Francisco and the North Bay. Then, in the late 1800's, an incubator was perfected here which would make Petaluma famous as the "Egg Basket of the World." Almost everyone raised chickens, and millions of eggs were shipped each year around the globe. After the poultry industry declined in the 1940's, dairying became the area's prime industry, remaining so until the suburban surge of the 1960's and '70's.

The story of the town would not be complete without a mention of the McNear family, who played an important role in Petaluma's economy for nearly 100 years. John McNear came to Petaluma with his wife in 1856, and was joined a few years later by his brother George. Together they established a shipping business and built grain warehouses along the river. In 1874 George moved to the East Bay and set about developing the grain trade at Port Costa, while John expanded his interests in Petaluma to banking, railroads and flour mills. His son, George Plummer McNear, continued the family tradition with a feed mill empire that served the emerging egg industry. Over the years, the McNears also donated land for a cemetery, park, fire station, school, and country club.

ᐦᐧ᠑ **Begin your ride** of Petaluma at Walnut Park, located at the intersection of Petaluma Boulevard and D Street. If you are coming from San Francisco on Highway 101, you will find the park by taking Petaluma Boulevard South into town. From the north, exit onto Washington Street. Go left at Petaluma Boulevard to D Street and the park. (Restrooms are available here.)

Known as The Plaza when laid out in 1873, Walnut Park was given its present name in 1896 by the newly formed Ladies' Improvement Club, who created the pleasant landscaped square you see today. The president of the club was Mrs. Henry Atwater, who lived across from the park in the beautiful 1875 Italianate house at #218 Fourth Street.

From Walnut Park, ride left onto D Street, which passes through one of the finest residential neighborhoods in town. The numerous historic homes here cover the years from 1865 to 1930 and encompass a wide range of sizes and styles. First you will see a large double-turreted duplex, at #411, built about 1870. Even older is the small cottage on the next block, at #519, dating from 1865.

The 1925 Spanish Revival dwelling at #600 was designed by Julia Morgan, architect of Hearst Castle at San Simeon. An especially distinctive residence is found at #758. This Queen Anne was built in 1890 for H. T. Fairbanks, a successful gold miner. The house at #853 with the unusual brick work dates from 1902. Local architect Brainerd Jones designed the home at #901 with its columns and verandas. It, too, was built in 1902. On the other side of the street, at #920, is another Queen Anne from the 1870's. It belonged to the Bihn family, owners of one of the largest hatcheries in the state.

Turn right at the next corner onto Laurel Avenue. In one block, make a right on B Street, heading toward the downtown area. Although not as grand as the D Street residences, this avenue has several interesting old houses also, such as the 1870 Queen Anne at #827 and the ornate Georgian Revival residence at #619 from 1907. In contrast is the modest home at #523, built in 1860 in the Greek Revival style.

The church at the other end of the block, at the corner of B and Fifth Street, was originally constructed in 1901 as the First Congregational Church. Since 1965, it has been the Evangelical Free Church. Across Fifth Street is a 1911 primary school designed by Brainerd Jones, now the school system administration office.

Beyond Fourth Street, traffic on B is often congested, especially on weekends, so you may want to see this area on foot. A few short blocks ahead, at the end of B Street, is the Great Petaluma Mill, located on the Petaluma River. When George P. McNear built a large feed mill here in 1902, he incorporated some earlier warehouses into the structure, one possibly dating back to 1854. The mill was saved from demolition in 1975 and has been converted into a lively complex of restaurants and specialty shops.

From the corner of Fourth and B Street, turn onto the one way. Here is the **Carnegie Free Library**, built of local sandstone in 1904 with funds donated by Andrew Carnegie. Also designed by Brainerd Jones, this elegant Classical Revival structure features a beautiful stained glass dome. Serving as Petaluma's public library until 1976, it now houses the historical museum, open Thursday through Sunday, from 1:00 to 4:00 pm.

On the other side of the street is an elaborate ironfront building constructed by John McNear in 1886. Don't miss the moustached faces above each window. This is just one of a number of such decorative ironfront structures still found in Petaluma.

McNear Ironfront Building

In the 19th century, builders often used cast iron elements to strengthen and embellish the facades of brick or wooden buildings. The pieces were cast at a foundry and then bolted onto the underlying structure. Cast iron facades were thought to be extremely strong and fireproof, but this illusion was dispelled by the 1906 earthquake and fire, which destroyed virtually all of San Francisco's countless ironfronts. Fortunately, Petaluma's buildings were spared by the earthquake and later by urban renewal.

At the end of the block on the right, you will go by another iron-front, the bright blue **Mutual Relief Building**. It was the home of a community life insurance cooperative, which provided $2000 in death benefits to the survivors of its members.

For a better view, make a left turn on Western, and stop at the corner. From here you can see the row of ironfronts which are considered Petaluma's greatest architectural treasure. The Mutual Relief Building dates from 1885. The smaller structures beyond were saloons, two of the 42 that existed in town in 1886. At the far corner of the block is the three-story Masonic Building, erected in 1882 at the height of Petaluma's river-centered prosperity. The town clock sits on top. Together, these buildings are unmatched anywhere in California as examples of a once-popular style.

Additional ironfronts are located on Petaluma Boulevard and Kentucky Street (the continuation of Fourth). These are best viewed on foot, however, as these streets bustle with activity, making relaxed bicycling difficult. Perhaps you have already noticed the I.O.O.F (International Order of Odd Fellows) Building on Petaluma Boulevard on your way to Walnut Park. It dates from the 1870's.

Leaving the commercial downtown area, ride on Western 2 blocks to Liberty. Turn right here, watching for the drainage ditch at the corner. As you head up the hill, you will pass two nicely restored 1890's cottages on the left, the first of several attractive Victorian residences you will see in this part of town.

In the next block, at #226, is an elaborate three-story Queen Anne home built in 1902 for Lyman C. Byce, the inventor of the world's first practical egg incubator. This invention in 1879 paved the way for the emergence of Petaluma's poultry industry, which dominated the town's economy for years.

By the turn of the century "chicken farming" was widespread, with 90% of the people living near Petaluma raising chickens. In 1923 the world's only chicken pharmacy opened. The chicken and egg business began its decline only after World War II, when high labor and feed costs forced thousands of small chicken farms into the hands of a few large producers.

Continuing past the Byce house, make a right turn at the corner onto Prospect Street. #200, the large Queen Anne at the end of the block, was constructed in 1892, shortly after Mrs. William Brown, a widow with eight children, married the owner of one of the saloons on Western Avenue. As you turn left on Keller, note the beautiful stained glass windows. These are from a local funeral home and were added more recently. More lovely Victorian residences are found on Keller. The Stick style house at #311 dates from 1871. Amid the homes is the 1927 Philip Sweed School, another design by the prolific Brainerd Jones. #343 on the corner, built in 1892 for a popular dentist, overlooks the Petaluma River.

Continue on Keller to its end at West Street, turning left. In two blocks go right on Keokuk, riding downhill to Magnolia Avenue, where you go left. Although the road has no shoulder, there is generally room for both bicycles and passing automobiles.

Very soon you will come to the entrance of Cypress Hill Cemetery, the final resting place for members of the McNear family. John NcNear donated land for this cemetery after the death of his 29-year old wife Clara. John and Clara had five sons, but only one, George Plummer, lived to adulthood. The circular family plot is located on the highest hill in the far left corner, marked by a white obelisk. Here Clara, John and their children are buried, along with John's second wife Hattie and other McNears.

Past the cemetery, you will ride by a mixture of older farm houses and newer residences, as Magnolia, with its gently rolling hills, gradually takes you away from town and into Petaluma's countryside. In less than a mile, turn right onto Marshall. Watch for abandoned chicken coops along the route, remnants of the town's chicken raising heyday. Soon Marshall ends at Skillman Lane.

If you are doing the shorter route to the Petaluma Adobe, turn right here. The optional side trip goes left into open ranch land toward the Washoe House.

Optional side trip: *Ride left on Skillman Lane, away from Petaluma, for nearly two miles. When you reach a stop sign, follow Skillman left to Bodega Avenue. To the left across Bodega is the tiny 1891 Holy Ghost Church. Turn right on Bodega, which has fast-moving traffic but a wide shoulder. The first right, in less than a mile, brings you onto quiet King Road. When King ends in 1.5 miles, go left onto Pepper Road. Now you are in dairy country; the farms are larger and the hills more open.*

About half a mile further along, on the left, just past the next intersection with Pepper Lane, you will see a yellow farmhouse, where Luther Burbank was first employed in Sonoma County; in 1876, he went to work for W. H. Pepper as a nurseryman. The Pepper ranch later was home to the famed race horse Kenilworth, winner of 94 major races.

After riding a little more than a mile, turn right on Mecham Road, named for Harrison Mecham, owner of much of the land grant Rancho Roblar de las Miseria. He came to Petaluma in 1853 and became a rancher of enormous wealth, power and influence. Although a respected member of the community, he had a reputation for violence, once shooting a man who persisted in taking a shortcut across his property. Unshaded Mecham Road has the longest climb of the ride, but it is less than a mile and not very steep.

When Mecham ends, make a left turn onto Stony Point Road. This was once the stage road between Santa Rosa and Petaluma, and it still carries fast-moving traffic. Just ahead, at the intersection with Roblar Road, is the **Washoe House**, among the oldest continually operating roadhouses in California and all that is left of a small community once located here. Built as a stage coach stop in 1859, it continues to offer food and drink to travelers.

Washoe House

From the Washoe House, return toward town on Stony Point Road, continuing past Mecham. After 2 miles, go right on Jewett Road, a pleasant shady country lane. Cross Pepper, going straight ahead on Center Road. After Center angles left, it joins Liberty Road. A small cemetery is located at this intersection, built on land donated by Mecham. He and his family are buried here.

Follow Liberty to the right as it takes you back to Skillman, where you go left. In 2 miles, when Marshall intersects from the right, you will have rejoined the main route of the ride.

Main route continues: Ride on Skillman for half a mile. As you near the intersection with Petaluma Boulevard North, note the Cinnabar Performing Arts Theater, up the hill behind the red barn on the right. It is located in a 1914 Mission Revival style school building. (A store/restaurant can be found on the left.)

As you cross Petaluma Boulevard at the traffic light, the road becomes Corona Road, which takes you up and over Highway 101 and then back into farm country. In a little more than a mile, make a right turn at the stop sign onto Ely Road. There are wide expanses of open fields here, protected from development, at least for the time being, by Petaluma's limited growth policy. Ride on Ely about 3.5 miles, passing from rural to suburban surroundings. After crossing Washington and Caulfield, make a left turn at Casa Grande Road, in order to reach the adobe home of General Mariano Vallejo.

Soon, you will see the large structure ahead at the end of Casa Grande. To reach the entrance of **Petaluma Adobe State Historic Park**, go right on Adobe Road a short distance. If you plan to tour the grounds, open 10:00 am to 5:00 pm, be sure to bring a lock, as you must leave your bicycle at the parking lot. Picnic tables and restrooms are located nearby.

In 1834 the Mexican government sent General Vallejo to Sonoma to establish a military garrison. He was also granted Rancho Petaluma, an area of 44,000 acres. In 1836 he began work here on the rancho's main building. Although never completed after ten years of construction, the adobe was nearly twice as large as it is today.

Cattle raising, the main activity of the rancho, was easy and profitable in this area of mild climate and rich grasslands. Hides and tallow were traded to foreign merchants for goods manufactured in other parts of the world. Ranch workers also raised horses, sheep and grain crops.

In 1846 the Bear Flag Revolt in Sonoma brought an end to the rancho's great period of prosperity. While General Vallejo was being held prisoner, the ranch was stripped of its livestock and supplies. Indian laborers left and did not return. In 1857, Vallejo sold the adobe and surrounding land. After years of neglect, the adobe was restored and is now a National Historic Landmark. A visit here gives one a good impression of what life was like during rancho days.

Leaving the Petaluma Adobe, retrace your route. On Casa Grande, just after the grove of eucalyptus trees on the right, look for an old one-

Petaluma Adobe

room school house that still has its flagpole. At Ely Boulevard, go right, and in less than a mile, make a left onto Caulfield, using the left turn lane. Follow Caulfield back over Highway 101, making a right on Payran Street. From Payran, go left at Jefferson, one block before busy D Street. At the end of the road is the Sunset Line & Twine Company, housed in an 1892 red brick factory building resembling a New England mill from the 1870's. Until 1929, this was the Petaluma Silk Mill, where silk from China was made into thread and hosiery. The left wing and tower were added in 1922.

Ride on Erwin to D Street, where you go left over the railroad tracks. This busy road takes you through an industrial area and over the 1933 drawbridge that crosses the Petaluma River. This is the most congested part of the ride.

One block after Petaluma Boulevard (Walnut Park is on the left), make a right onto Fourth Street. The 1932 post office on the corner is situated where the spacious mansion of John and Hattie McNear once stood. Go left at C Street to St. John's Episcopal Church at the next intersection. This fascinating building with its tower and spires was designed by British architect Edward Coxhead in 1870.

In another block, go left again onto Sixth Street. Of special interest here is #100, a 1901 Colonial Revival home built for William Lewis, owner of Borjorques Ranch, one of the largest dairy ranches in northern California.

Continue on Sixth, crossing D Street. The attractive Eastlake Stick style home at #312, with its colorfully painted detail, was built in 1882 by State Senator A. P. Whitney as a wedding present for his oldest son. The handsome 1862 Victorian farmhouse next door, at #320, belonged to the senator, who had a very successful grocery business.

At the end of the block, go left on F Street. This takes you by a small 1870 church at Fifth, as well as other old houses. In another block, a left at Fourth brings you back to Walnut Park, the end of your tour of Petaluma, a town that is justly proud of both its Victorian architecture and rural heritage.

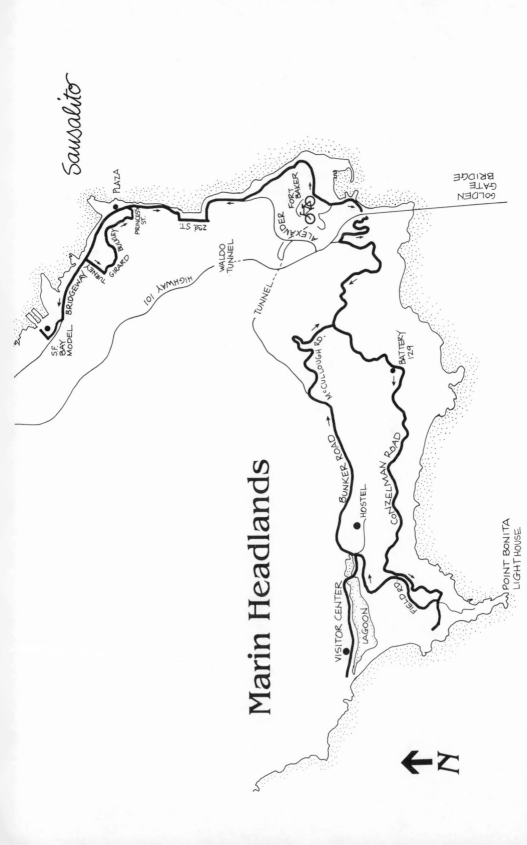

Marin Headlands

Sausalito

N

Marin Headlands

Distance: 14 miles with 7 mile optional addition

Rating: Some sustained climbs, narrow roads, and heavy weekend traffic near the Golden Gate Bridge all make this a **strenuous** ride, one for experienced cyclists only. Due to the absence of shade, it may be hot in summer on sections away from ocean breezes. An ideal time to do the ride is in early spring when the Headlands are green and wildflowers are blooming. There are no stores or restaurants on the main route. The optional extension to Sausalito has some short, steep hills and congested streets. It is rated **moderately strenuous**.

Highlights: This ride offers the chance to explore remnants of coastal defense fortifications representing several historic periods, from Civil War days to the age of nuclear missiles. You will also have spectacular views of San Francisco, the Headlands, Golden Gate Bridge, and the ocean, especially on a clear day. Sausalito, destination of the optional segment, is known for its impressive bay vistas, elegant shops and galleries, fine restaurants, and historic landmarks.

In the latter part of the 19th century, the San Francisco harbor defense system was expanded across the bay to the Marin Headlands. Numerous gun emplacements were embedded into the coastal hillsides as a means of protecting the harbor from foreign naval attack. With the threat of air bombardment after World War I, batteries of anti-aircraft guns were added to the defense system. In the 1950's two Nike ground-to-air missile silos were installed in response to more advanced military technology. Fortunately, none of these fortifications was ever needed to repel enemy attack, but their existence has saved the land on which they stand from urban sprawl. This grassy, windswept open space is now part of the Golden Gate National Recreation Area (GGNRA).

Begin your ride at Fort Baker, located beneath the north end of the Golden Gate Bridge. To reach the fort by car from San Francisco, cross the bridge and take the Alexander Avenue exit. Drive past the turn off to 101 South, which heads back to the city, and make the next left, following the signs to GGNRA and Forts Cronkhite, Baker and

Barry. (From the north, take the last Sausalito exit.) Immediately before the tunnel, go right on Bunker Road, curving back under Alexander Avenue and down to Fort Baker. Turn right on Murray Circle, and park at the south end of the open parade grounds. (Pit toilets are located near the fishing pier and at several other locations on the route.)

Fort Baker, a subpost of the Presidio of San Francisco, began as Lime Point Military Reservation when part of Rancho Saucelito was sold to the United States Government in 1866. A permanent fort was established at Horseshoe Bay in 1897 and named for Colonel Edward Dickinson Baker, a Civil War hero and friend of Abraham Lincoln. Once several thousand men were stationed here, residing in the picturesque white structures surrounding the parade grounds. Today, the fort is quiet and nearly empty.

From the parking lot, ride back to the junction of Murray Circle and the narrow road heading left toward the bay. This is the beginning of Conzelman Road, which will take you first along Horseshoe Bay, with its fishing pier and views of the Presidio Yacht Harbor, and then beneath the Golden Gate Bridge looming overhead. The winding road climbs less than a mile to the intersection with the main part of Conzelman, where you go left and continue uphill. This section is steep, often with heavy traffic and little shoulder, but it is short. At the top of the rise, on the left side of the road, is Battery Spencer, built in 1896. It is one of the earliest Marin military installations. Walk your bicycle back off the road to see all of the buildings in the complex and to take in the fine views of the Golden Gate Bridge, Fort Baker and San Francisco.

The road continues uphill more gradually for another 1.5 miles, passing McCullough Road. At the very top is **Battery 129**, an unfinished World War II construction. This fortification was to have been armed with two massive 16-inch diameter guns, which could accurately fire a distance of 25 miles. The project was terminated in the mid-1940's, however, when it was realized that the guns would be ineffective against the enemy aircraft of the day. It later became the site of a Nike radar station. Today, it is also known as Hawk Hill, for the numerous species often sighted soaring overhead.

Ride through the first tunnel of the battery to see one of the gun mounts and to enjoy a view of Point Bonita and the rest of Conzelman Road. Notice, too, the trees here. Battery 129 would have been the highest artillery battery in the Bay Area, and the trees were planted to "camouflage" it. (As you continue your ride, you will see that practically the only trees on the Headlands are those planted at battery sites.)

Conzelman becomes one-way past the battery. The downhill is very steep (12% grade) but with good surface, little traffic, and thrilling views of Point Bonita and its lighthouse. After the road flattens out, you will come to Battery Rathbone-McIndoe, completed in 1905. In its early years it was fitted with rapid fire rifles to protect the entrance to the bay from enemy ships. During World War II, it guarded the mine fields located outside the Golden Gate Bridge. The guns were removed in 1948.

Conzelman Road

At this point, the road heads down again, although not so steeply. At the bottom of the hill, turn left toward Point Bonita. Climb up to Battery Wallace, built in 1919 as part of the naval defense system but later modified to guard against air attack. Again, notice the trees planted as camouflage, now providing shade for the picnic area.

After a downhill, go left at the YMCA Outdoor Center and past the road leading to the Point Bonita Lighthouse. The first lighthouse was constructed in 1855 on the cliffs above the present site. It was rebuilt in 1877 on the rocks below for better visibility in fog. It is open for regularly scheduled tours. (Call the Marin Headlands Visitor Center at 415-331-1540 for information.)

Ride on to Battery Mendel, completed in 1905 and used until 1943. It was named for Colonel George Mendel, an engineer who designed many of the military structures in the Bay Area. From here you have a view of the Battery Wallace gun mounts. A short distance beyond the battery is Bird Rock Overlook with its view of Rodeo Lagoon, named for the rodeos held there when the Headlands were part of Rancho Saucelito, the Mexican land grant awarded to William Richardson.

Return past the lighthouse entrance, riding by the YMCA buildings and warehouses on Field Road. On the other side of Battery Alexander is a 1955 fenced underground Nike missile site. It housed both a 60-mile range Ajax missile and a 75-mile range Hercules before being dismantled in 1974. The site is closed to visitors except for scheduled ranger-led tours. (Call the visitor center for further information.)

At the bottom of the hill, Bodsworth Road on the right leads to the Golden Gate Hostel at Fort Barry. The hostel is located a short distance away in what was once the officers quarters of the fort. The building dates from 1902 and is a pleasant place to stay if you have made this ride part of an overnight trip. Call 415-331-2777 for reservations.

At the end of Field Road, a left turn onto Bunker Road will take you to Fort Cronkhite and popular Rodeo Beach. Here you will also find the **Marin Headlands Visitor Center** where you can learn about the natural history of the area. (Water and restrooms are located adjacent to the parking lot.)

Retrace your route past the visitor center. Before leaving, you may wish to visit the California Marine Mammal Center, located just off Bunker Road. It is housed in another Nike site.

Continue on Bunker about 2 miles until McCullough Road enters on the right. You must turn here, as bicycles are not allowed in the Bunker Road tunnel ahead. Climb one mile up McCullough, turning left at the top onto Conzelman. A stop here before the mile-long downhill will provide one last breathtaking view of San Francisco and the Golden Gate Bridge. Remember the steep hill just past Battery Spencer, and use caution. Make the right turn just before the bottom of the hill, following the bike route sign, to return the way you came.

If you want to add a ride across the Golden Gate Bridge, one entrance to the west side (for weekend riding) is through the parking lot on the left. There, too, is the pedestrian walkway under the bridge which leads to Vista Point and the bay side of the bridge (for weekday riding). A second entrance to the west side can be reached from a road on the right, a short distance down Conzelman. (The ride across the Golden Gate Bridge is described in the chapter on San Francisco.)

Follow Conzelman Road back under the bridge to Fort Baker to end your tour of this historic part of our nation's seacoast defense system.

Optional addition: A visit to Sausalito will provide an interesting change of pace, as well as a wide choice of sustenance for hungry cyclists. To do this side trip, ride past your starting point, going right on East Road. After a short uphill, you will have grand views of Angel Island and the Tiburon Peninsula. In one mile, turn right before the subway, following the Pacific Coast bike route sign. This brings you to Alexander Avenue, the busy and narrow route down to Sausalito. Follow the road through several turns, and soon you will be on Bridgeway, the main street of town.

*The history of **Sausalito** goes back to the days of Captain William Richardson, an Englishman who arrived at San Francisco Bay in 1822. He married the daughter of the commander of the Presidio, was appointed captain of the Port of Yerba Buena (which would become the city of San Francisco), and established the first civilian settlement there. In 1838 the Mexican governor awarded him Rancho Saucelito ("little willows"), a land grant of over 19,000 acres, and he moved his family here. Richardson operated schooners that carried passengers and freight between Sausalito and Yerba Buena, served as justice of the peace, and built the Sausalito Water Works, which supplied water for the city across the bay. For many years Richardson prospered, but eventually he went heavily into debt trying to prove title to his land grant. When he died in 1856, most of his estate went to his lawyer, Samuel Throckmorton.*

The town itself began in 1868 with the formation of the Sausalito Land & Ferry Company, a partnership of San Francisco businessmen who purchased three miles of waterfront property from Throckmorton and divided it up into lots. Expanded ferry service and the completion of the North Pacific Coast Railway in 1875 brought new settlers to Sausalito—laborers, merchants and wealthy entrepreneurs. Mansions were built on the hillsides, and the town soon became a popular destination for weekend excursions.

By 1900, however, gambling interests had taken over, bringing all kinds of trouble and corruption. "Undesirables" from San Francisco arrived by ferry, saloons became the scene of drunken brawls, and even city officials were involved, collecting pay-offs from the gambling houses. Although efforts to clean up the area and eliminate political corruption by the Sausalito Woman's Club achieved some success, Prohibition brought more illicit activity in the form of bootlegging. The picturesque town you see today, with its art galleries, elegant boutiques, upscale restaurants, and yacht clubs is hardly recognizable as the rough and tumble place it used to be.

As you ride along Bridgeway, you will have the waterfront of Richardson Bay on one side and the hills, crowded with homes and apartments of all sizes and styles, on the other. Ahead, on the right, is the former San Francisco Yacht Club building, now the location of two restaurants, including the well-known Ondine's. The yacht club helped make Sausalito a major recreation center when it moved its headquarters to the town in 1878. The present structure dates from 1898. The building beyond was formerly a launch service in use from 1907 to 1937. It, too, is now a restaurant.

*You will pass more restaurants and numerous shops as you continue to the downtown area. Stop a moment when you reach **Plaza Viña del Mar**, a small park guarded by two concrete elephants. These statues once held 100-foot flagpoles at the 1915 Panama Pacific International Exposition in San Francisco and are a popular sight in Sausalito. The fountain is also from the exposition. The park was created by land-fill in 1904.*

Plaza Viña del Mar

Located behind the park at the end of El Portal is the ferry dock. Here one can board ferries to San Francisco's Fisherman's Wharf (Red and White Fleet, 415-546-2896) or to the Ferry Building (Golden Gate Ferry Service, 415-982-8834). To the right of the park on El Portal is the Sausalito Hotel, which has been offering hospitality since 1910.

The streets of Sausalito may seem crowded with automobiles today, especially on weekends, but imagine the traffic jams that occurred in the 1920's when ferries were the only means of reaching San Francisco. Although two ferry companies were in operation, they could not keep up with the huge numbers of travelers. On one summer weekend in 1926, the ferries carried over 70,000 automobiles. The construction of the Golden Gate Bridge in 1937 finally relieved Sausalito's overburdened ferry lines.

On the other side of Bridgeway, near Anchor Street, is a brick building with second-story bay windows and decorative arches. Constructed in 1894 as a bank, it served as city hall from 1925 to 1974. (Public restrooms and telephones are located on the right a short distance past Anchor.)

As you continue down Bridgeway, you will pass Village Fair, a unique, multi-level shopping complex. This was once a parking garage for commuter automobiles during the 1920's ferry boat era. Next door is the Casa Madrona Hotel and Restaurant. The original structure, located up the hill, was built in 1885 as the private residence of William Barrett, a wealthy lumber baron. Today, with numerous additions extending down to the main street, it is a lovely inn.

If Bridgeway traffic is heavy, you may wish to ride on the bike path, which begins at Johnson Street. When the path ends in 6 blocks at Napa, return to the roadway, taking the next right down Marinship Way. In a short distance, turn right to reach the entrance of the U. S. Army Corps of Engineers **Bay Model***, a hydraulic scale-model of the entire San Francisco Bay and Delta. The huge model provides a scientific means of analyzing the effects of change on the Bay and Delta. It is open free of charge Tuesday to Saturday, from 9:00 am to 4:00 pm. During the summer, it is open Tuesday to Friday, from 9:00 am to 4:00 pm, and Saturday and Sunday from 10:00 am to 6:00 pm. Here you may also see the 1915 freighter Wapama in drydock on the bay. This historic steam schooner is slowly being restored. (Restrooms can be found outside the Bay Model entrance.)*

The Bay Model is located in what was once the main warehouse of Marinship, a 200-acre shipyard for building World War II cargo vessels. Although boatbuilding has been a continuous activity in Sausalito since Richardson's day, nothing before or after can compare to Marinship. Almost overnight, a huge shipyard complex sprang up, bringing in many thousands of workers. The first Liberty ship, named the William A. Richardson, was built and launched in September 1942, just six months after shipyard construction was begun. In three and a half years of service, Marinship produced 15 Liberty cargo ships, 78 oil tankers and 20 invasion barges. With the end of the war, Marinship closed its doors, and Sausalito was quiet once again.

The former shipyards now house an industrial complex and several marinas. Nearby you will also find the famous Sausalito houseboat colony, begun in the 1950's by local artists and writers. In spite of the city's efforts to discourage them, these early bohemians used old boats and ferries as their homes and studios. Today, these picturesque floating dwellings, ranging from elegant to derelict, are an established part of Sausalito.

From the Bay Model, go back the way you came. Ride up to Bridgeway and turn left. The route takes you past Litho Street, where city offices, a library, and the Sausalito Historical Society Museum are located in a 1927 high school building. The museum is open Monday, Wednesday, and Saturday, from 10:00 am to 1:00 pm. In another 2 blocks, make a right turn on Turney Avenue, heading uphill.

At the corner of Bonita Street, on the right, is the Sylva Mansion, built in 1897 for Adolphe Sylva, a pro-gambling mayor at the turn of the century. In the 1930's, after the structure was converted to a boarding house, bank robber Baby Face Nelson, who had escaped from an Illinois prison, stayed here under an assumed name. William Richardson's 1841 adobe hacienda was once located near this intersection but has long since disappeared.

In one block, a left turn will bring you onto Girard. There on the corner, at #47, is the 1869 Gardner House, the oldest residence in Sausalito that remains in its original condition. It was built for former South Carolina Senator James Gardner and is a typical Victorian Gothic cottage with bargeboard trim and split columned porch.

Follow Girard, using caution on this narrow road as you cross intersections. Traffic moves rapidly coming up the steep streets and is often hard to see until it crests the hill. As you ride, you will have fine views of the harbor and Richardson Bay.

At San Carlos, go straight on Bulkey Avenue, the most level of the streets ahead. At #156 Bulkey is the upper entrance to Casa Madrona, which you saw from Bridgeway. The house at #140 is unusual in that it evolved from a water tank into a striking tower residence. It dates from around 1900.

The First Presbyterian Church, at #100, is a 1909 brown shingle structure with a distinctive entrance arch and redwood interior. This was also the site of the founding of the Sausalito's Woman's Club, started to save a cypress tree from being cut down by developers.

From the church you can see the Alta Mira Hotel across the street, built in 1927 to replace an earlier structure destroyed by fire. To the left of the hotel is Laneside, an 1892 home built by Henry Campbell as a wedding gift for his wife. It has undergone considerable remodeling over the years and is now part of a housing complex.

Next door to the church is Villa Ladera, previously the home of Lorenzo Scatena, who died one month after its completion in 1930. Scatena was one of the founders of Bank of Italy, which today is known as Bank of America. He was president until 1915, when his stepson Amadeo Giannini took over. The elegant Mediterranean-style structure with its ornate entrance gate is now condominiums.

Follow Bulkey downhill as it becomes Princess Street, named for the first ferry that ran from Sausalito to San Francisco. From here you will have an especially good view of the other side of Villa Ladera.

More turn-of-the-century commercial structures are located in this area, including the brick Becker Building on Bridgeway at the intersection with Princess. Built in 1897 as a store and newsstand, it has distinctive cast-iron detailing on the second floor.

Make a right turn on Bridgeway if you are ready to leave Sausalito. At the end of Bridgeway, just as the road goes right, is the 1902 twin turreted Castle by the Sea, once a saloon and hotel. Note one last historic building before you leave town. The Chart House-Valhalla Restaurant is located on the left off Second Street. Built in 1893 as a German beer-garden called Walhalla, it was reopened as Valhalla in 1950 by Sally Stanford, former San Francisco madam.

Continue up the steep hill on Alexander Avenue. Just outside Sausalito, take the first right, following the bike route sign, which will take you through the subway beneath Alexander. From here, retrace your route back to the starting point. Along the way, you will be rewarded with more spectacular views of Alcatraz, the Bay Bridge and San Francisco.

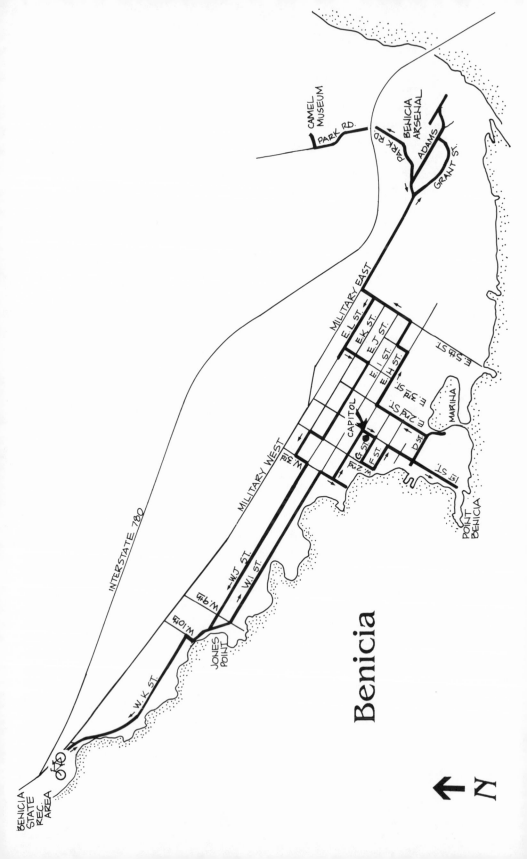

Benicia

Distance: 12 miles

Rating: This **moderate** route is mostly flat to rolling with some short uphill climbs. Following lightly traveled city streets, it is a ride that enthusiastic beginners might also enjoy. This is a good excursion any time of year, as the westerly winds off the Carquinez Strait bring cooling breezes even on a hot summer day. (These breezes, however, may become strong headwinds on your return trip.)

Highlights: Benicia is a delightful town with lots of history to explore, including a former state capitol and the pre-Civil War era federal arsenal. In addition, part of the ride follows peaceful Carquinez Strait, and offers views of tankers and freighters on their way to Port Benicia.

When Benicia was established in 1847, it was expected to become California's leading city, the commercial and maritime rival of nearby San Francisco. The chief founders were Dr. Robert Semple, who had participated in the Bear Flag Revolt in Sonoma, and his partner Thomas O. Larkin. Impressed with the beautiful Carquinez Strait as a possible site for a city, Semple negotiated with imprisoned General Mariano Vallejo for donation of the land, part of the General's vast estate.

Semple suggested the new town be named Francisca, after Vallejo's wife. But when the town of Yerba Buena across the bay changed its name to San Francisco, Semple renamed the new city Benicia, one of Mrs. Vallejo's other names.

Located in a position to command both ocean and interior waterway navigation, the town quickly attracted a number of settlers. By 1850 when it, along with Monterey, became one of the first two cities to be incorporated in the newly formed state of California, its population had grown to 1,000.

Benicia, however, never reached the expectations of its founders. By World War I, its growth had slowed, as San Francisco became the major city of northern California. Today, the central part of Benicia still looks much as it did in the early part of the century.

Begin your ride at the Benicia State Recreation Area east side parking lot, next to the Carquinez Strait. It is located off Interstate 780 at the Military West exit.

Leave the parking lot, turning right on West K Street. This route follows the strait and goes by an assortment of old and new homes, as well as piers and fishing docks. The city of Benicia has constructed a series of waterfront parks which add to the pleasure of the ride. You will pass the first of these little parks at the foot of West Twelfth Street.

At West Tenth Street, turn right to find the entrance to a bike path which leads to the larger Ninth Street Park at Jones Point. Here, about a mile from the start of the ride, are a swimming beach, boat-launching ramp, restrooms, and a monument to Commodore Jones for whom the point is named.

Leave the park by way of West I Street. At West Fifth, ride on the paved pathway ahead and then on a gravel road, coming back onto West I in a block. A right turn at West Third will take you by some early Benicia homes. The Victorian at #715 has been beautifully restored. The big house across the street is a plain Eastlake style with a magnificent view of the water.

Return up Third, going right on West H Street. Notice the charming cottages at #267 and #257 on the left. They are identical except for slightly different trim. Here also is the site of the 1849 Peabody Hospital, the first hospital to be established in the West.

Benicia Capitol

Continue on H Street to First Street, the main street of Benicia, where you will find several restaurants, stores and antique shops, many located in early 1900's commercial structures. Turn right and then right again in one block. On the corner with West G Street is the **Old State Capitol Building**, the most noteworthy and prominent structure from Benicia's pioneer days.

This two-story brick building was constructed in 1852. Ostensibly intended as the city hall, it was promptly offered to the state as a capitol building. The offer was accepted, and in 1853 Benicia became the third capital of the State of California (after San Jose and Vallejo). Just one year later, the capital made its final move to Sacramento.

In the years since, this dignified building, designed to resemble a Greek temple, has been used for a variety of purposes. It has housed a school, library, church, police station, fire department and city hall. Now, as the Benicia Capitol State Historical Park, it has been restored and furnished as it appeared during the period of legislative use. It is open daily from 10:00 am to 5:00 pm.

The **Fischer-Hanlon House** next door is equally as interesting. This handsome residence was once a hotel on First Street. It was purchased by Joseph Fischer in 1856 and moved to this site. After renovations and additions, it was occupied by generations of the Fischer family until donated to the state in 1969. The house is open for docent-led tours on weekends from noon to 4:00 pm. You may visit the gardens at any time.

Continue on G Street, turning left on West Second and then onto the bike path. At its end is another tiny park with excellent views across the strait to the rolling hillsides beyond.

From the park take West F Street back to First Street, turning right. At #401 is the Union Hotel, dating from 1882. It is an inn and restaurant. Across D Street is the Washington House, an 1850 wharf building which was moved to this site and remodeled as a hotel. At various times in the past, it served as a bordello, speakeasy and Chinese lottery but now accomodates more conventional tenants.

Turn right on West D Street to reach an old saltbox house at #145. It was prefabricated in the East and shipped to California to be reassembled at this location. It dates from the gold rush days.

Return to First Street, going right. As you continue riding toward the water, traffic is light and buildings fewer in number, but once this area was teeming with activity. The first ferry across the strait was established nearby in 1847 by Dr. Semple. Ferry service between Benicia and Martinez was in continuous operation for 115 years until the highway bridge was completed in 1962.

The end of First Street was the location of the transcontinental train ferry dock. The ferries that operated here were the largest in the world, carrying an average of 30 Southern Pacific trains across the water daily. Service between Benicia and Port Costa was in operation from 1879 to 1929 when the railroad bridge was constructed.

Benicia was a relay station for the Pony Express system during the short time it operated in 1860-61. A sign marking the site can be found at the corner of First and A Streets. The waterfront was also the site of the first canneries in Solano County, and several tanneries were located here as well. At one time Benicia was the principal leather processing center of the Pacific Coast.

Little remains today to evoke the past. Point Benicia is now just a fishing pier, and the only buildings left are the 1900 railroad depot and delapidated Jurgensen's Saloon, a favorite haunt of author Jack London when he lived on a houseboat along the waterfront. These structures are being considered for restoration as part of the Historic Triangle waterfront area.

Return up First, turning right on East D Street with its several well-preserved early residences. At its end, cross the street to the marked bike path adjacent to the yacht club. Follow the path to the right for a glimpse of the new 309-berth marina. (Restrooms can be found in the building where the store is located.) Almost deserted during the week, this area hums with activity on a summer weekend. The marina, condominiums and planned commercial development signal changing times for Benicia.

Leaving the marina, go right on East Second Street away from the waterfront. Before turning right on East H, notice the red brick office building on the corner. The oldest section, facing H Street, is the 1877 Benicia Powerhouse. In 2 blocks, turn left on East Fourth and then, at the next intersection, take a right on East I Street. On your left is St. Dominic's Church. The first Catholic church was built on this site in 1852. The present building dates from 1890.

From I Street, turn left onto East Fifth Street, and then, at the traffic light, go right onto Military East. This thoroughfare becomes Grant Street in half a mile as you enter the **Benicia Arsenal**, now the Benicia Industrial Park.

The Benicia Barracks, established in 1849, became the first arsenal on the Pacific coast two years later. Although the importance of the Benicia military post was superseded in later years by the San Francisco Presidio, it served the needs of the U. S. military until its closing in 1964. Gun powder and cannonballs and, later, high explosives were stored here. Among its most famous soldiers were the young lieutenants Ulysses S. Grant and William Tecumseh Sherman.

In the Civil War era, the arsenal was a staging area for western troops. The last of its garrisoned soldiers was sent to the Philippines at the time of the Spanish-American War, but the importance of the arsenal continued. During the World Wars and the Korean War, it served as Pacific Coast ordnance headquarters.

Many of the arsenal's historic military buildings have been preserved and can be visited today. As you enter the Industrial Park, the first you will see is the large mission style arsenal headquarters building dating from World War II. It now houses the offices of the park. Ride by on Grant, staying to the right. At this point the road narrows.

Continuing on Grant, you will soon arrive at the Bachelor Officers' Quarters, located on the left at #983, just after the road crosses a short bridge. This two-story stone building with its columned porch dates from 1872. A short distance up the road at #1060 is the old Command Post, built in 1870.

Go right onto Adams Street, then take an immediate left up the short hill on Washington Street, leading to Johansen Square and Commandant's Lane. Stay to the right to visit the **Clock Tower Fortress**, built in 1859 to command Carquinez Strait and protect the post from possible Indian attacks. Originally the sandstone building had a third story and a second tower, but both were destroyed by an accidental explosion in 1912. When the fortress was rebuilt, the clock was added as a memorial to Colonel Julian McAllister, commander of the Arsenal for 25 years. Before leaving, you will want to take time to enjoy the fine views of the Port of Benicia and the bridge over the strait.

From the Clock Tower, a ride through the parking lot will bring you to the imposing Commandant's Home. This 20-room mansion of classic Georgian design dates from 1860 and was once a social center for Bay Area society. From 1906 to 1911 Stephen Vincent Benet lived here while his father was commanding officer of the post.

Ride downhill and turn right on Adams, going past the 1872 guardhouse on the left. Make a right turn on Park Road, a short steep uphill, following the road under Interstate 780, as you head toward more old arsenal buildings.

In just over half a mile, go right on Camel Road, following the signs to the **Camel Museum**. There you will see two long sandstone buildings, constructed in 1853 and 1854 for use as warehouses. They are more popularly known as the Camel Barns, however, for the brief period in 1863 when they were used to stable a herd of camels. The animals had been imported in 1856 by the government as an experiment in the transportation of military supplies across the southwest desert. When the camels proved unsatisfactory, they were driven to

Benicia and sold at auction. The Benicia Historical Museum is now located here and is open weekends from 1:00 to 4:00 pm. From April through September, it is also open on Fridays.

A narrow gravel road leads away from the barns down toward the Powder Magazine, built in 1857 of local sandstone. Behind the four-foot thick walls of this building designed to store powder are hand-carved Corinthian pillars and graceful vaulted ceilings. It is generally open to the public at the same time as the museum.

Follow Park back to the bottom of the hill, where you go right on Adams. Adams rejoins Grant, which soon becomes Military East again, as you leave the arsenal. A left turn at the traffic light brings you back onto East Fifth Street.

In one block go right on East L Street. Across from the brick city hall, at #235, is Captain Walch's Home, built in 1849. His house, now privately owned and sadly neglected, was one of three identical dwellings built in Boston, dismantled, shipped around the Horn, and reassembled here. A second house was sold in San Francisco and no longer exists. The third became Lachryma Montis, the residence of General Mariano Vallejo in Sonoma.

Captain Walch's Home

Turn around, going right at the corner onto East Third Street, which takes you past the old Benicia Primary School. Make a right turn at the next corner, East J Street, noticing the interesting houses in the next block. At #120 on the left is St. Paul's Rectory. This typical New

England saltbox house was originally built in Connecticut in 1790. It was purchased in 1868 by Captain Julian McAllister, later arsenal commander, who had the house disassembled and shipped around the Horn to be rebuilt at its present site. Two rooms were added the following year.

Next to the rectory, on the corner of East J and First Streets, is the Gothic style St. Paul's Episcopal Church. Dating from 1859, this is the oldest Espiscopal church in California. Work on the building was done by shipwrights, and the arched ceiling resembles the inverted hull of a ship. The bell tower was added in 1863. The beautiful redwood interior and stained glass windows can only be seen when the church is open for services on Sunday and Wednesday.

Continue on J Street, crossing First Street. At #110 West J Street is the first Masonic Temple built in the State of California. Constructed in 1850, the two-story frame building is currently a Masonic museum. Turn right on West Second Street to West K Street.

To the right is the City Park, site of the first Protestant church in California, built in 1849. Across the park, at #160 Military West, is the Benicia Fire Museum. On display are antique fire extinguishers and fire engines, including California's first. The museum is open weekends from 9:00 am to 5:00 pm, June through October.

Beyond the park was the location of St. Catherine's convent and school. Established in 1854, it provided education for many young pioneer ladies until it moved to San Rafael to become Dominican College. Benicia was also the site of several other educational institutions. In 1855 the first law school in California was established here. The Benicia Seminary, founded in 1852, was an early Protestant girls' school and the forerunner of Mills College, now located in Oakland.

A left turn onto West K Street will bring you to the Ridell-Fish house, one of the largest and most impressive residences in Benicia. Located at #245, it is notable for its Queen Anne architecture and wrought iron fence. At the next intersection go left on West Third, and then right on West J Street.

At the end of J Street, in less than a mile, is the Ninth Street Park and the beginning of the bike path. From here, retrace your route back to the starting point, concluding your tour of this historic waterfront town.

At this point, you may wish to do still more riding. If so, take the mile-long bike path from the other side of the parking lot to the main part of the recreation area. You can then follow the road another mile to Dillon Point. With all it has to offer, Benicia is definitely a town worth knowing.

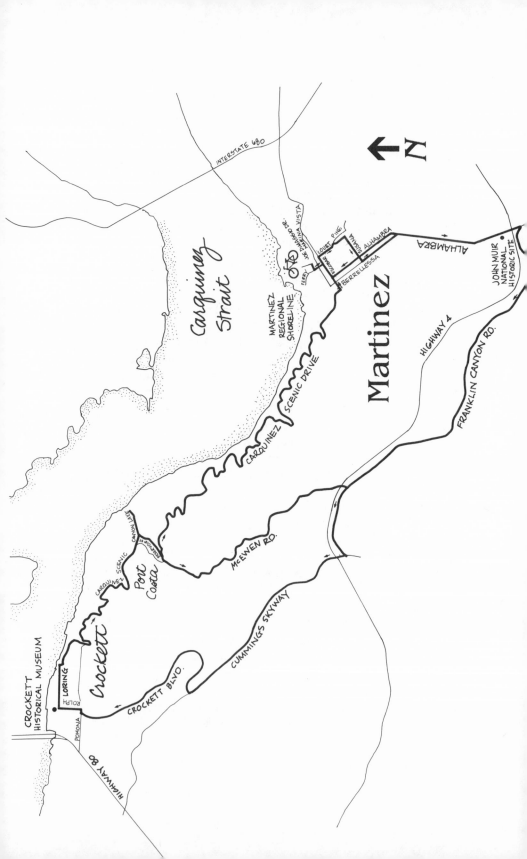

Martinez

Distance: 22 or 25 miles

Rating: The hills outside Martinez make this a **strenuous** ride, although the city streets are flat. The return route also involves either some rough, broken pavement or a very steep climb. There may be traffic in the city, but the open country roads are lightly traveled. This ride is particularly enjoyable in spring when the hills are green and the poppies are in bloom.

Highlights: This ride takes you back to a time when shipping activity filled Carquinez Strait and to the towns that are reminders of those early days. In Martinez you will visit the home of John Muir, famed conservationist and founder of the Sierra Club. The route to Crockett and Port Costa offers wonderful views of the countryside and Carquinez Strait.

Carquinez Strait, the waterway connecting the Sacramento River with the San Francisco Bay, became a major route of commercial shipping during the second half of the 19th century, resulting in the development of several waterfront towns. Grain from the Central Valley was brought by boat and railroad to ports along the Strait on the way to be shipped to markets in San Francisco and Europe. Ferries carried both passengers and trains across the Strait to the northern part of the state. Sugar and oil refineries were built. The bustling waterfront was crowded with warehouses and wharfs, ships and railroads, hotels and saloons.

Begin your ride at Martinez Regional Shoreline, a popular recreational area that bears little resemblance to the time when ferries, ships, and fishing boats lined its waterfront. To reach the park from Interstate 680, take Marina Vista to Ferry Street, going right to the park entrance on Joe DiMaggio Drive. The park has miles of nature trails, an exercise course, a horse arena, soccer fields, and picnic areas. There are even bocce ball courts that recall the predominantly Sicilian population of the shoreline's early days. The softball complex is named for Martinez native, Joe DiMaggio, who played for the New York Yankees. A marina and fishing pier are located at the end of the road. With all this activity, the park is likely to be a busy place, especially on summer weekends. Try parking in the first lot on the left. (Restrooms can be found nearby.)

The town of Martinez, named for the original Spanish land grantee, was laid out in 1849 and designated the county seat of Contra Costa County the following year. Its location on the Strait soon made it an important grain shipping port. After the railroad reached Martinez in 1878, shipping became the town's major industry; both local and Central Valley agricultural products were sent to San Francisco, Europe and elsewhere. Warehouses lined the waterfront all the way to Port Costa, and the area swarmed with thousands of railroad men, sailors, teamsters, and stevedores.

By 1885 the railroad and wharves of Port Costa carried most of the grain crops to market, and grain shipping at Martinez declined. Other industries gradually took its place, however. Local orchard crops continued to be loaded at the Martinez docks. Commercial fishing expanded when two fish canneries were established. In the late 1890's, manufacturing also added to the town's growth. The first oil company arrived in 1895, followed by the Royal Dutch Shell Oil Company in 1914. This was Shell's first refinery in the United States. The Alhambra Water Company started bottling pure mineral water in Martinez in 1903.

Martinez remained an important business center until the 1930's, when the ease of transportation to the larger cities of Oakland and San Francisco took its toll. Today, many think of the city only in the terms of the oil refineries that can be seen from Interstate 680. But Martinez and its surrounding countryside have much more to offer.

Leaving the park, you will ride by the Amtrack Railroad Station. Although considerably altered, this is the same depot built by the Northern Railway Company in 1877. As you cross the tracks, imagine the congestion in the days when grain shipping, by rail and boat, was a million dollar industry. Now only a few trains pass through each day.

Continue on Ferry Street, crossing Marina Vista into the downtown area. The oldest commercial buildings here date only from the first part of the century, as earlier structures were destroyed in disastrous fires in 1894 and 1904.

Turn left in one block on Escobar to reach the **Martinez Museum** at the corner of Escobar and Court Streets. The museum is located in a two-story cottage built in 1890 for Dr. J. S. Moore as his residence and dental office. It is now the home of the Martinez Historical Society and has a fine collection of local memorabilia. It is open free of charge Tuesday and Thursday from 11:30 am to 3:00 pm, and the first and third Sunday each month from 1:00 to 4:00 pm.

From the museum, go up Court Street past the County Finance Building. Constructed in 1901 as the court house, its original dome was removed for earthquake safety in 1957. Other county structures along this street replaced fine homes and mansions in what was once the city's elite residential district.

In a short distance, just as the road curves left and bcomes Pine Street, make a right turn to stay on Court. This takes you away from the government buildings and into a neighborhood of old homes. When you reach Susana Street, named for Susana Martinez Smith, wife of the founder of the city, go right. Just on the other side of Alhambra Creek is a small, tree-shaded park with restrooms.

Susana ends in one more block at the plaza donated by the Martinez family in 1849. To the left is the Boys and Girls Club, housed in a much-altered 1909 grammar school. To the right is the Martinez City Hall and Police Department built in 1916 as the grammar school annex. Ride through the park and cross one-way Alhambra Avenue. At the next corner, go left onto one-way Berrellessa. Although there is often heavy traffic, this street is wide enough for both cars and bicycles.

Soon Berrellessa merges with Alhambra. You will pass the grounds of the Merrithew Memorial County Hospital on the right. Set back off the road is the oldest of the hospital buildings, dating from 1910. Ride along Alhambra for a little over a mile to the **John Muir National Historic Site**, open daily from 10:00 am to 4:30 pm.

John Muir House

John Muir was born in Scotland in 1838 but came to the United States in 1849, eventually making his way to California. Most of his life was spent exploring, studying and writing about the great mountains of California and Alaska, their valleys, glaciers and wildlife. Many of the mountain peaks and glaciers up and down the Pacific coast were discovered and named by him. In 1880 he met and married Louie Strenzel of Martinez.

The large Victorian home you see here on the hill was built in 1882 for Dr. John Strenzel, Muir's father-in-law. Strenzel was a colorful figure in his own right, having been a Polish revolutionary, medical doctor, Texas frontiersman, and Forty-Niner before settling down as a successful fruit rancher in the Alhambra Valley. Muir, who lived about a mile away with Louie and their two daughters, joined his father-in-law in the orchard business. When Dr. Strenzel died in 1890, the Muirs moved into this home.

Soon afterwards, John Muir retired as an orchardist and returned to his travels, especially into his beloved High Sierra, devoting the rest of his life to the fight to save America's vanishing wilderness. His prolific writings were highly influential in establishing conservation of natural resources as national policy. He was also one of the founders of the Sierra Club in 1892 and served as its president until his death. Muir felt his greatest accomplishment was the part he played in the creation of Yosemite National Park in 1906. His most bitter disappointment came in 1913 when he was unable to save the beautiful Hetch Hetchy valley from being dammed for a reservoir. He died one year later.

To visit the John Muir home and grounds, enter through the visitor center (restrooms are located here). Ask a ranger to open the locked gate, so you may safely leave your bicycle on the other side of the fence. Of special interest in the house is Muir's study, where he wrote so many books and articles, and the displays highlighting the history of the Sierra Club. From the bell tower you will see that the view of Martinez has changed considerably from Muir's day. You might wonder what he would think of the highway overpass, busy roads, and commercial establishments nearby. After touring the house, take the orchard walk past the carriage house to the **Martinez Adobe**.

In 1824 Ignacio Martinez, the Commandante of the San Francisco Presidio, was granted Rancho El Pinole, a large parcel of land stretching from Alhambra Creek in present-day Martinez to Point Pinole to the west. At his death in 1848, the land was divided among his children. Vincente Martinez built this adobe in 1849 on his portion of the inheritance. The house was sold four years later to Edward Franklin, for whom Franklin Canyon is named.

Dr. Strenzel bought the adobe and surrounding land in 1874 and planted fruit and nut trees. The structure became a storehouse and residence for ranch employees. Many years later, it served as the home of Muir's daughter, Wanda, and her husband.

When you have finished exploring these fascinating dwellings, it is time to leave Martinez and ride the hills to Crockett and Port Costa.

From the Muir Site, go right on Alhambra and beneath Highway 4. Just on the other side, turn right onto Franklin Canyon Road. This takes you away from the traffic of the city and into the quiet countryside. The first part of the road is narrow and mostly level, as you ride by homes, farms and ranches. Gradually you climb higher, while the trees disappear and the shoulder widens. After 3.5 miles, McEwen Road to Port Costa intersects on the right. (This is the alternate return route.) The section past this point is a little steeper but less than a mile long. When you reach the top of Franklin Canyon Road, go right on Cummings Skyway over Highway 4. Enjoy the views of the open grassy hills as you climb another 1.5 miles. On the left, you can see the Bay and, if the day is clear, Mt. Tamalpais beyond. As you start down the other side, watch for a right turn in half a mile onto Crockett Boulevard. This is an exhilarating 2-mile downhill with little traffic, a high point of the ride.

Crockett Boulevard ends at Pomona Street and the town of **Crockett**. To your left is the red brick John Swett High School, named for the man known as the father of California schools for his part in developing the state's public school system. His ranch was located in nearby Alhambra Valley. The Carquinez Bridge (Interstate 80) dominates your view past the school. Its southbound span dates from 1926.

Go right on Pomona and immediately left on Rolph Avenue. At the end of the street is the massive **C & H Sugar Refining Plant**, the center of Crockett's economy since 1906. Here also is the Crockett Historical Museum, located in the former railroad depot. It is open Wednesday and Saturday, from 10:00 am to 4:00 pm, and is free.

The beginnings of Crockett date to 1865 when lawyer and later judge John B. Crockett received a strip of land along the Strait in payment of legal fees. He offered a partnership in the land to Thomas Edwards, who became the first settler. In 1880 Edwards purchased part of Crockett's share, and Dr. John Strenzel of Martinez bought the remainder. Edwards laid out a town on his land, naming it Crockett. Strenzel laid out another town to the west, which he called Valona. Both towns grew and prospered during the heydays of shipping, but only Crockett remains today.

C & H Sugar Refining Plant

The Old Homestead, the Edwards family residence, can be found under the tall palm trees in the far corner of the parking lot across from the museum. Dating from 1867, it is the oldest home in Crockett. It is now the Women's Community House.

The first factory in Crockett was located on the present site of the C & H plant when John Heald began manufacturing farm machinery here in 1881. The following year Abraham Starr constructed a huge flour mill next to Heald's plant. In 1897 Starr's mill was converted to sugar beet refining by George McNear from Petaluma, but this venture was not successful. McNear then leased the mill to the Spreckel's sugar interests who reopened the plant in 1906 to refine Hawaiian cane sugar. The California and Hawaiian Sugar Refining Company has been in operation ever since and is the largest sugar mill in the world. This refinery site was chosen partly because ships bringing sugar cane from Hawaii can dock directly beside the mill. Once refined, the sugar is distributed by the railroad whose tracks run next to the factory.

Over the years, C & H has provided many services for the town, including a public library, sewers, road improvements, a men's club, parks, and a swimming pool. Crockett became known as a company town, and most of the residents were C & H employees. During the first quarter century, business was brisk, and the town thrived. Even during the Depression, all C & H workers who were heads of households kept their jobs. But times changed, and the first of several strikes by the refinery workers union was called in 1935. World War II and automation brought further modifications in the work force and working conditions. Eventually, as new highways provided quick access to other areas, fewer and fewer employees actually lived in Crockett. C & H gradually decreased its financial support of the town, which now manages all its own expenses.

To leave Crockett, follow Loring Avenue uphill away from the bridge. This was once a busy street, lined with stores and saloons serving factory workers and longshoremen. Now container ships have eliminated the need for the longshoremen, and residents go elsewhere to shop, leaving many of Crockett's buildings empty and dilapidated. Past the I.O.O.F. building, however, are several nicely maintained old homes with wonderful waterfront views.

Loring Avenue goes right onto Vallejo. In a block, turn left on Winslow Street, which follows the Strait and then takes you up and out of town. When you reach Carquinez Scenic Drive, the continuation of Pomona Street, go left toward Port Costa. This road dates to 1886 and was once part of the state highway system.

After about 1.5 miles of scenic rolling hills, angle left onto Canyon Lake Road through the tiny town of **Port Costa**. Note the beautiful little church up the hill to your right. St Patrick's Catholic Church was built in 1893 and is open for services each Sunday at 11:00 am. The town's main street is only a few blocks long and ends at a large parking lot near the Strait.

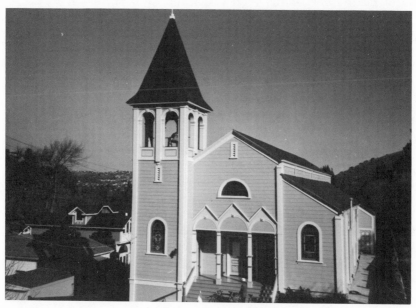

St. Patrick's Catholic Church

It is hard to believe that Port Costa was once the largest wheat port in the world. The town was first established in 1878 as a terminal for the Central Pacific Railroad ferry. This 420-foot boat could carry 32 freight cars and a locomotive across the Strait. The port then became the principal grain-loading facility for hundreds of square-rigged sailing ships from all over the world. Although the town never had more than 300 permanent residents, there were as many as 3000 sailors, railroad employees and stevedores here at the height of the grain-shipping season. Several hotels and numerous bars were built to accommodate them. Brawls were frequent and violence not uncommon, as hundreds of workers were hemmed into a town only two streets wide.

Tracks, piers and ferry docks occupied the flatland of Port Costa, while homes were constructed on the hillside. The town flourished until 1930 when the railroad bridge connecting Martinez and Benicia opened and ferry service was ended. About this time, also, the river channel to Sacramento and Stockton was deepened. As a result, steamers loaded their cargoes directly at those ports, and trains went through Port Costa without stopping. In 1941 all usable piers burned and were never rebuilt.

Little is left from this early time. The buildings that once lined the waterfront are gone. The stone **McNear Warehouse** still stands, however, after surviving four fires and two earthquakes. It was built in 1886 to store wheat, hay and potatoes and was the first fireproof building in Contra Costa County. Today it houses a cafe. Across the street, the 1870's hotel still offers visitors a place to spend the night. The stone restaurant next to the hotel dates from 1897. On weekends, tourists visit Port Costa's antique shops and restaurants, enjoying the quaint ambiance. Muriel's Doll Museum, located at 33 Canyon Lake Drive, is another attraction. Open 10:00 am to 5:00 pm, Tuesday through Sunday, the museum has hundreds of antique dolls on display.

Return up Canyon Lake Drive, and at the school building, go left onto Reservoir Street. This short steep uphill brings you back to Carquinez Scenic Drive.

At this point you must decide how you wish to return to Martinez. Carquinez Scenic Drive to your left is beautiful; it follows the Strait about 5 miles over rolling hills with wonderful views of the water and the Benicia bridge in the distance. However, there is a one-mile section that is closed to automobiles because of landslides. While this results in little traffic on the road, it also means you will have two places where the pavement has fallen away, and you may have to walk your bike. Other road hazards include broken glass, gravel and rocks. The route is popular with bicyclists, but the county warns that you ride this road at your own risk.

Your other choice is to cross Carquinez Scenic Drive, going straight ahead on McEwen Road for 2.5 miles. This lightly traveled road is also scenic but narrow, and involves a very steep climb of less than a mile. The road then widens, and the climb is more gradual. After a mile-long downhill, McEwen brings you back to Franklin Canyon Road, where you go left, back down to Alhambra Avenue. Turn left here, following Alhambra about 2 miles to Escobar in downtown Martinez. To see the Tennent and Tucker homes (described below), go left. To return to Shoreline Park, make a right turn. At Ferry Street, a left turn takes you back to your starting point. The McEwen Road alternative is about 3 miles longer than the route along Carquinez Strait.

If you follow Carquinez Scenic Drive, you will go by Port Costa Materials in a mile. The company has been making bricks at this location since 1906. In another mile is a barrier, which marks the beginning of the mile-long closed section. In addition to watching for road hazards, be aware that motocyclists also use this road. After the second barrier, you will have one last climb to reach the pioneer cemeteries of Martinez. At the top of the hill on the left is the Alhambra Cemetery, final resting place of most of the county's founders. Dating from 1854, it is the earliest burial ground in the county. Across the road is the cemetery of St. Catherine's Parish, begun in 1873. Here lie many of the early rancho families, including Martinez children and grandchildren.

The downhill from the cemeteries takes you onto Talbart Street and by several early cottages. Two larger homes can be seen in a few blocks at Escobar. On the corner of Escobar and Talbart is the 1888 Queen Anne of Dr. John Tennent, a Martinez descendent. Up Escobar to the right, at #110, is Captain Tucker's house, one of the handsomest in town. It was built in 1877 in the Italianate style.

From the Tucker house, ride downhill, continuing on Escobar through the downtown area. At Ferry Street, go left, back to Shoreline Park. Before leaving Martinez, you might want to ride down to the marina and fishing pier to see how the shoreline has changed since the days when ships, ferries and trains crowded the waterfront.

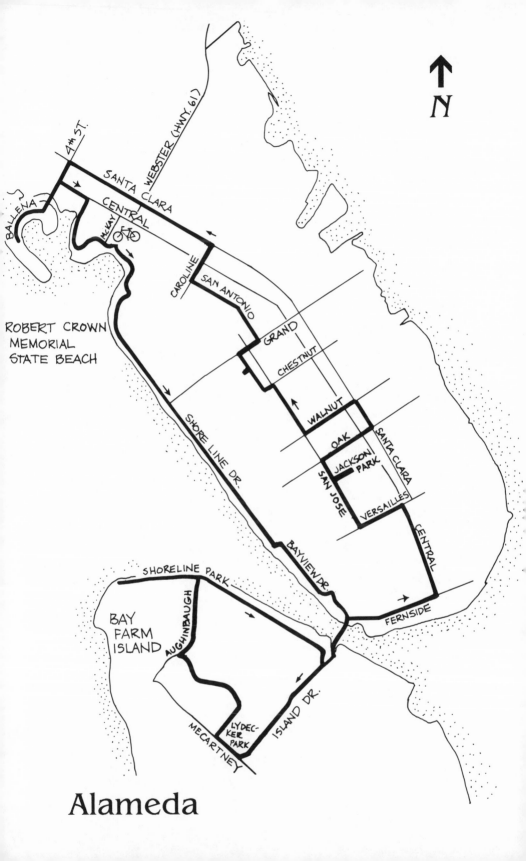

Alameda

Alameda

Distance: 10 miles with 4 mile optional side trip

Rating: This ride is flat and **easy**, taking place on bike paths, bike lanes, and quiet city streets. There are only a few busy intersections to cross and the possibility of congestion along the bike path on a summer weekend.

Highlights: Alameda is known for its Victorian architecture, and you will see a wonderful variety here, ranging from small cottages to "Gold Coast" mansions in a suburban setting. Riding along the shore, you will also have spectacular views of San Francisco Bay. The side trip to Bay Farm Island adds more wonderful vistas.

Alameda, one of the East Bay's oldest cities, was built on land originally settled by Costanoan Indians. Granted to Antonio Peralta in 1820, the area became Rancho Encinal de San Antonio and was used for cattle grazing. American development began in 1851 when the rancho was purchased by Gideon Aughinbaugh and W. W. Chipman. To attract new residents, the developers ran a small steamer from San Francisco, offering Sunday excursions, watermelon picnics and free lots to anyone who would erect a $50 building. In 1853, with over 100 settlers, the town of Alameda was founded in the southern part of the island. Two other towns were also laid out—one called Woodstock at the opposite end, and one at the center named Encinal.

Population grew slowly until the 1870's when major railroad lines arrived in the area and regular ferry service across the Bay was instituted. The next decade saw the town's greatest period of development. Described in real estate brochures as an ideal bedroom community, Alameda claimed to provide "healthful climate, perfect sewage, park-like drives, charming homes, pure artesian well water, and pleasant, convenient rail and ferry service." Today there are nearly 2800 surviving buildings dating from before 1905.

The availability of water transportation also attracted many large industries, including shipbuilding yards and cannery warehouses. During World War II seven naval shipyards operated in the city. The demand for homes was great and soon all available land was covered with tract housing. Despite this war time boom, Alameda retains a pleasant Victorian residential atmosphere.

🚲 **Begin your ride** at Crab Cove Visitor Center, part of Robert W. Crown Memorial Beach. To reach Alameda from Highway 880, take the Broadway exit and follow signs to Alameda/Highway 61. This will bring you through the Webster Street tunnel. When Webster ends at the other side of the island, turn right on Central, and take an immediate left onto narrow McKay Avenue. The visitor center is located here. Parking is free, although the lot fills quickly on a summer weekend. (If you are bicycling to Alameda, you will have to cross the channel on Fruitvale Avenue, 23rd Street, or High Street.)

The visitor center is open Wednesday through Sunday, 10:00 am to 4:30 pm, March through November. It is closed during the winter. It houses a collection of historic Alameda photographs as well as displays on marine life. Restrooms are located behind the building and are open all year.

From the 1870's to the 1930's, this area was the site of amusement parks, swimming pools, elegant resort hotels, restaurants, and bars. Neptune Beach was created in the early 1900's, adding a dance pavilion, boardwalk, stadium, skating rink, merry-go-round, and roller coaster. There was even a 100-foot high entrance gate in the shape of a Moorish tower. This "Coney Island of the West" was enormously popular until changing times brought about bankruptcy in the late 1930's.

Nothing is left from this era except Croll's Bar, located at the intersection of Webster and Central. Dating from 1879, the mansard-roofed structure is one of Alameda's most interesting old commercial buildings. A saloon was first installed in 1883, and the original bar, brass railings, and beveled mirrors remain intact. At the turn of the century, the upstairs was used as a rooming house by several boxers who trained across the street at Croll's Neptune Gardens, part of Neptune Beach amusement park. Perhaps the most famous of these fighters was heavyweight champion James "Gentleman Jim" Corbett.

During World War II, the military took over the beach and turned it into a maritime training center. The structure that houses the visitor center was a military hospital, and the brown maintenance building beyond was the training center itself. The beach became a state park in 1959 and is now managed by the East Bay Regional Park District. Long known as Alameda Beach, it was renamed for the state legislator who helped gain its state park status.

From the visitor center, go left along the bike trail that follows Crab Cove, a marine reserve. The path soon brings you to the main part of Crown Beach. At the bath house, the path turns inland toward a large parking lot. Continue to the right as the path divides; this will bring you back along the water, as you follow Shore Line Drive toward the other end of Alameda Island. Here you will have enjoyable views across San Francisco Bay and of Bay Farm Island ahead. This whole section of Alameda was actually part of the bay until filled in during the 1960's. Sand has been trucked in to create the beach you see today, providing a pleasant environment for both people and wildlife.

When Shore Line ends, stay on the paved bike trail as it curves left along Broadway. At the corner, turn right on Bayview Drive, and ride along the street. When you reach Otis Drive at the traffic signal, go right onto the sidewalk, which soon becomes a wide paved path leading to the Bay Farm Island Bridge. Cross Peach. If you plan to do the optional side trip to Bay Farm Island, continue along the path toward the left, up to the bridge. To stay on the main route, go to the right, following the path under the bridge.

*Optional side trip: When you reach the bridge, walk your bike along the sidewalk over the channel separating the two islands. On the other side, ride straight ahead on the marked bike path which parallels Island Drive, watching for cars as you cross side streets and entrances to the shopping center. All the land to your right has been created by bay-fill and is rapidly being developed. Once **Bay Farm Island** had many truck farms growing produce for San Francisco. Now the farms are gone, replaced by golf courses and the Oakland airport.*

At Mecartney Road, follow the bike path right, around the corner. Pass the main entrance to Lydecker Park, turning right onto another paved path between the ball field and tennis courts. When you reach the lagoons constructed as part of the housing developments, go left for a quiet ride along the waterways. The numerous ducks, egrets, and other water fowl here don't seem to mind that this is not a natural habitat.

When the bike path reaches the street, make a right turn, following Aughinbaugh Way. At its end, cross Sea View Parkway to pick up another trail that runs the length of Shoreline Park. Here you will discover new views of San Francisco, Alameda, and the Marin Headlands. To the left, the paved path ends in half a mile, although plans call for it eventually to continue around the island. Follow the path to the right until it returns to Island Drive. At Island, go left on the path up to the bridge, and again walk your bike across the west side of the bridge.

On the Alameda side, take a left onto the bike path as you ride off the bridge. Stay to the left, going under the bridge. You have now rejoined the main route.

Main route continues: Follow the path to a point where you can exit onto Fernside Boulevard. Soon you will have a bike lane as you ride along the eastern end of the island.

In about half a mile, make a left turn at Central Avenue, where you will see some of the many Victorians for which Alameda is known. The land to the right, however, just beyond Central, was not developed until the 20th century. Before that it was Fernside, the great estate of A. A. Cohen, owner of a ferry service from San Francisco. His three-story, 70 room mansion had an art gallery and 5000 volume library. It burned to the ground in 1897.

When you reach Versailles Avenue in several blocks, go left. In the next block, at #1238, is the oldest house still standing in Alameda. Built in 1854 for J. N. Webster, a San Francisco money broker, it is believed to be a pre-fab shipped around Cape Horn. Its charming Carpenter Gothic style with "icicle" trim is unaltered except for the exterior shingles. It is now a bed and breakfast establishment, as well as a coffee shop, open Wednesday to Sunday, 10:00 am to 3:00 pm.

Continue on Versailles to the corner, turning right on San Jose. In a few blocks is Jackson Park, surrounded by a number of well-preserved Victorian homes from the 1880's and 90's. On the other side of Park Avenue East, turn right onto the path that runs the length of the park.

As you circle around this half of the park, try to imagine what life was like when this tract was developed in the late 19th century. When you have finished admiring the homes here, continue along San Jose. In another block you cross Park Street. Park was the center of the town of Encinal and has been the heart of Alameda's business district since the 1890's.

Just past Park, turn right on Oak Street. In several more blocks you will find the **Alameda Historical Museum**, on the left behind Alameda High School. It is open Wednesday to Sunday from 1:30 to 4:00 pm, and Saturday from 11:00 am to 4:00 pm. The school itself, which faces Central, is also worth examining. The dignified building with its long row of Ionic columns dates from 1926.

On the other side of Central is the impressive Twin Towers Methodist Church. This building was constructed in 1909, although the church was founded much earlier, in 1853. At the next corner, turn left on Santa Clara. On your right is the 1896 City Hall, of Romanesque design. Its 60-foot central clock tower was damaged in the 1906 earthquake and eventually removed. Across the street is the Alameda Free Library, built in 1902 with funds donated by Andrew Carnegie.

Continuing on Santa Clara to the next corner, make a left turn on Walnut. In several blocks, a right will bring you back onto San Jose Avenue once again. This part of town was known as the "Gold Coast" during Alameda's most prosperous decades, from 1870-1900, because of the many large and lavishly decorated homes constucted here.

Gold Coast Mansion

The most elaborate structures are located at the next intersection and are among the finest Alameda has to offer. The one on the right, #2103, was built in 1891 for George Brown who made his money in San Francisco real estate. The larger one at #2070 dates from 1893 and was the home of David Brehaut, a contractor. This incredible residence used every ornamental motif popular at that time on its multi-textured facade. It is hard to believe that each of these Queen Anne-style homes was built at a cost of about $4000.

At the next intersection, turn left on Chestnut and then right at the corner to Clinton. In 2 blocks go left down Union Street to see several more impressive homes from the 1890's. John Leonard, one of Alameda's most productive architect-builders lived in the 1896 shingled dwelling with the tower at the end of the street, #891. Built at a cost of $20,000, no expense was spared on its interior detail, and it was one of the earliest houses wired for incandescent lighting.

When originally developed, these lots were located on the bay, but Alameda's south shoreline has changed drastically since the Victorian era. The land you see on the other side of the estuary has all been created by bay-fill, and these homes have lost their wonderful views.

Continue along Clinton for another block to Grand Avenue. Before turning right on Grand, look left across the street to see an ornate Queen Anne from 1890. As you go right, note the 1879 Italianate on the corner.

Grand Avenue is another area known for its fine homes. After riding along it for 2 blocks, go left at San Antonio Avenue. At the next corner, don't miss the superb detail of the house on the left. It dates from 1889.

There is another residence of note several blocks further along San Antonio. The 1896 house at #1031 was the home of Major Charles Tilden, one of Alameda's most prominent citizens. The Classical Revival design of the house was copied at the owner's request from one in San Francisco, which was later destroyed in the 1906 fire.

Tilden House

At the next corner, turn right on Caroline Street, and when you reach Santa Clara Avenue, go left. After crossing busy Webster Street, ride on Santa Clara another 3 blocks. This end of Alameda has homes of a more modest size, but look for many of the same elaborate decorations found on the larger Victorians.

At Fourth Street, go left, crossing Central, and ride straight ahead through the Ballena Bay complex to the yacht club. From here you will have views of the U. S. Naval Air Station, which incorporated both an early Army field and the municipal airport. This is where the first China Clipper flight began in 1935, when the airport was the base for Pan American Airlines. Across the Bay you can see the San Francisco skyline.

Leaving Ballena, go right on Central a short distance. Watch for the bike path entrance on the right at the sign "Beach Access," just before Crown Drive. Follow this path along the water back to your starting point at the Crab Cove Visitor Center. This route has taken you by only a fraction of the many fascinating buildings in Alameda, so you may want to continue exploring the residential streets on your own. You might also want to stop at Croll's for a cool drink before leaving the fine old residential community of Alameda.

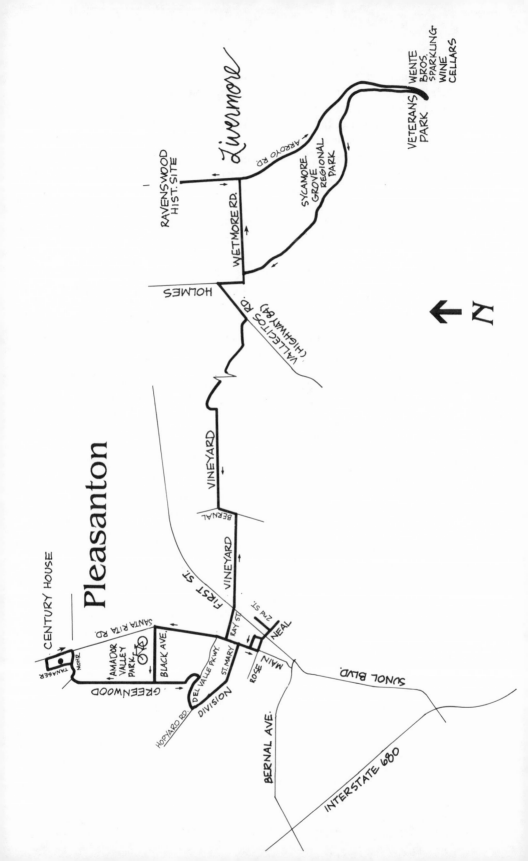

Pleasanton

Distance: 6 miles with 19 mile optional side trip

Rating: This flat route through the town of Pleasanton is **easy**, although traffic is sometimes heavy on Main Street. The optional side trip to Livermore is rated **moderate**; the rolling country roads often have little shoulder and there may be a headwind. It is especially enjoyable in spring, when the hills are green, or during fall grape harvests.

Highlights: Pleasanton is one of the fastest growing communities in the East Bay, but you can readily see its small town origins when you bicycle down Main Street and through surrounding neighborhoods. This ride includes a Victorian hotel and old adobe, as well as early commercial buildings and cottages. The route to Livermore offers views of still undeveloped countryside, along with visits to the Ravenswood estate and an historic winery.

The Amador-Livermore Valley was used for pasturing cattle by Mission San Jose after its founding in 1797. When the missions were disbanded in 1834, the area around what is now Pleasanton was granted to members of the Bernal family and was known as Rancho El Valle de San Jose. In 1850 Agostin Bernal became the first settler, building an adobe house which still stands on Foothill Road.

The man who was to become founder of Pleasanton, John Kottinger, arrived in Alisal, as the town was first known, in 1851. After marrying into the Bernal family, he established the first store and served as justice of the peace. He also mapped the town in 1867, renaming it Pleasonton in honor of his good friend Alfred Pleasonton, a Civil War general. The name became Pleasanton due to a clerking error.

The small town grew rapidly with the introduction of the railroad in 1869. By 1894 Pleasanton was the thriving center of an agricultural community of ranches, dairy farms, hop fields, and vineyards. Today most of the farm land has given way to suburban homes, shopping center development, and huge office and industrial complexes.

殳 **Begin your ride** through Pleasanton at the Amador Valley Community Park located at Santa Rita Road and Black Avenue. (Restrooms are located near the playground behind the Aquatic Center.)

From the park, ride west on Black Avenue (away from Santa Rita), taking the first right on Greenwood Road. In just over half a mile, Greenwood ends at Mohr, where you go right for one block and then left on Tanager Drive. This takes you behind Century House and Bicentennial Park, your destination. To reach the entrance, turn right on Sutter Gate Avenue and right again on Santa Rita. Since traffic is usually heavy here, you may want to use the sidewalk.

Century House was built in 1878 by George Atkinson as a hunting lodge. In subsequent years it was a farmhouse situated in the middle of open fields. Today this Gothic Revival-style building is surrounded by modern subdivisions, a contrast exemplifying the changes that have taken place as the town has grown. The house was restored and dedicated as part of Bicentennial Park in 1976, and is now operated by the City of Pleasanton as a rental facility.

Century House

After admiring the house and grounds, ride right on Santa Rita, using the sidewalk if traffic is heavy. At the corner, go right on Mohr, and then left on Greenwood, retracing your route. Continuing past Black, make a left turn at Harvest Road and a right at Del Valle Parkway.

The parkway ends at Hopyard Road. Once the area north of town had the largest hop fields in California, with much of the crop exported to London for ale-brewing. Turn left on Hopyard, using the sidewalk bike path to cross over the arroyo.

Hopyard immediately becomes Division Street, as you enter one of

Pleasanton's early residential neighborhoods. Division soon angles left onto St. Mary. The house at #443, across the railroad tracks, was constructed around 1880 by local architect Charles Bruce, who often chose floor plans from east coast pattern books and modified them to fit the small town's simpler style. This building was home to Charles Graham, a mortician, and his descendents, from 1900 to 1967. The charming little Queen Anne home next door, at #431, dates from 1895.

Turn right when you reach Main Street, which retains much of its small town ambiance even today. The metal "Pleasanton" sign over the street has been welcoming visitors since 1932.

At the far end of the block on the right is the Amador-Livermore Valley **Historical Society Museum**. The 1914 building has been used as the town hall, public library, and police department. The museum is open Wednesday through Friday, 11:00 am to 4:00 pm, weekends from 1:00 to 4:00 pm, and is free. The 1890's house next door once belonged to Jerome Arendt, a local businessman, and is now a restaurant.

Across the street is the 1890 Kolln Hardware building, probably the most recognizable landmark in town with its white corner tower. One of the small attached buildings facing Division Street was built in 1869.

Continue riding on Main Street for another block, and, before turning left on Neal, stop to see a pair of two-story brick commercial buildings, both dating from 1896. The Johnston Building on the right (corner of Rose) was originally a saddle shop and later a candy store. Currently, it houses an antique store. The structure across the street (on the corner of Neal), at #450, was Pleasanton's first mercantile establishment, operating as a general supply and dry goods store. Later it became a feed and grain business.

On the other corner of Neal and Main is the 1900 Arendt Building, once the location of the Bank of Pleasanton, as well as the post office and telephone exchange. You may have noticed the turret of a Victorian-style structure further down Main. Although it looks old, it actually was built only a few years ago, designed to fit in with the rest of Main Street's architecture.

Half a block down East Neal Street on the right is a white brick commercial building dating from the 1880's. Constructed as a family-run market with living quarters on the second floor, it has also been the location of a bank and the justice court. It has housed law offices for many years.

Across the railroad tracks is the newly renovated 1901 railroad station painted mustard yellow, the characteristic color of Southern Pacific properties. The second floor, once living quarters for the station master, is now offices. A coffee shop is on the lower level.

After crossing busy First Street, you will come to another residential section of town. At the next corner is the picturesque Amador Valley Baptist Church. Originally the Presbyterian Community Church, it dates from 1876. It was built on land purchased from Joshua Neal, who, like Kottinger, acquired property when he married a Bernal daughter.

Continue uphill on Neal to #303, an 1890's Queen Anne redwood home designed by Charles Bruce. The turret is of special interest; it contains a bedroom known as the Round Room.

Return down Neal, going right on Second to see more early homes. #4466 is a Gothic Revival house owned by the superintendent of the Southern Pacific Railroad. It dates from 1874. The one-story wings on either side were added later. On the next corner, at #4397, is one of the largest older homes left in Pleasanton. It was built for the Joseph Arendt family around 1890. Arendt was a wealthy downtown property owner. A little further on, surrounded by a white picket fence, is #4362, a Gothic Revival cottage that still has an old barn in back.

Turn around here, and bicycle back to Neal Street, going right, and once again cross First Street. Just after the railroad tracks, a right turn on Railroad Street takes you to the brick fire station, part of which dates from the 1920's. The bell in front was used to call volunteer firemen. Turn left in front of the fire station onto one-way Division Street.

Kottinger's Barn

At Main go right, and then take the second right onto Ray Street to see **Kottinger's Barn**, an adobe dating from 1852. It is located in the shopping center parking lot on the right and has been restored as an antique shop. When Kottinger was judge in Alisal, there were no funds for public buildings, so his home on Main Street was used as the courtroom and a corner of his barn served as the jail. An underground passage connected the two. Kottinger evidently was kept quite busy during the 1850's, when Pleasanton was known as "the most desperate town in the west." It was refuge for bandits who had ambushed prospectors returning from the gold fields, and Main Street shoot-outs were not uncommon.

If you plan to do the optional side trip to Livermore, continue along Ray Street. If you are doing the shorter route, turn around here.

Optional side trip: *Ray Street becomes Vineyard after crossing First Street and has a bike lane. At the stop sign in about .75 miles, follow the road left on Bernal, and then right, back onto Vineyard, an area of new subdivisions. Soon the developments end, and the road narrows, as you leave the city behind and pedal into the open countryside.*

Despite the lack of shoulder, the ride along this road is very pleasant, with views of fields, pasturelands, vineyards, and hills beyond. In about 4 miles, Vineyard ends at Vallecitos Road (Highway 84), where you go left a short distance. At the next intersection, make a sharp right turn onto Holmes Street, which becomes Wetmore as it turns left and goes by the entrance to Sycamore Grove Park.

The Livermore Valley, with its ideal growing conditions, has been home to vineyards and wineries for over 100 years. Before Prohibition, 15,000 acres of vineyards carpeted the valley floor. Although only 3000 acres remain, this is one of California's finest wine-producing areas.

In less than a mile, Wetmore ends at Arroyo Road. On your right is a stone entrance gate marked "Olivina," a remnant of the once great estate of Julius P. Smith. Smith and his brother developed a borax mining claim in Nevada into a product that eventually became Twenty Mule Team Borax. In 1884 he decided to use the money from the sale of his stock to establish a large winery in the Livermore Valley. Here he grew grapes, olives and nuts, and produced wine, olive oil and pickled walnuts. A large part of the estate is now Sycamore Grove Park.

Go left on Arroyo for half a mile to reach **Ravenswood Historic Site**. *This was once the country vineyard estate of San Francisco politician, Christopher Buckley. In 1885, the smaller Queen Anne cottage was constructed as living quarters for the Buckleys and their guests. The stable, carriage house and tank house, which included a* *kitchen, also date from that time. The bigger house was built in 1891 and used for parties and social gatherings.*

Buckley, an influential figure in the San Francisco Democratic Party in the 1870's and 1880's, was known as the Blind Boss. He was totally blind by the age of 30 as result of either a neurological disorder or excessive alcohol consumption as a youth. After his death in 1922, the property was sold to a Catholic order that intended to build a college on the site. The college was never realized, however, and in 1971 the land went to a developer. Most of the estate became a housing subdivision, but the acres where the buildings stand were given to the public and are maintained by the Livermore Area Park District. Ravenswood is now listed in the National Register of Historic Places. Although visible from the road, the grounds and buildings are presently open to the public only on Tuesday from 5:00 to 8:00 pm and for special events.

Return down Arroyo, continuing past the Olivina gate. From here, it is less than 2 miles to the Wente Brothers Sparkling Wine Cellars. The road is narrow, and there may be traffic, but the rolling hills are spectacular, especially in the fall when the grape vines turn red and gold.

Ravenswood Historic Site

The **Wente Cellars** *are located at what was once the historic Cresta Blanca Winery. Established in 1882 by Charles Wetmore, it was named for the white cliff above the vineyards. In 1889, a Cresta Blanca vintage was the first American wine to win an international gold medal, proving California could produce wines to compete with the finest in the world.*

Since 1981, the property has been owned by Wente Brothers, whose 1883 main winery is located on Tesla Road a few miles away. Several Cresta Blanca buildings are still in use, including the tasting room and century-old sandstone caves. The winery is open daily for tasting from 11:00 am to 5:00 pm, with tours on the hour. A gourmet restaurant is also located on the grounds.

Leaving the winery, go left to reach the entrance to Veterans Park across the road. (Restrooms can be found adjacent to the parking lot.) Here you will pick up a 2.5 mile bike path that starts at the far end of the parking lot. The path goes under the approach to the 1925 Veterans Administration Medical Center and then parallels Arroyo Road a short distance before turning left toward **Sycamore Grove Park**. *As you ride through this pleasant park, look for reminders of the once vast Olivina estate. You will pass an old almond orchard and several tree-lined avenues. In addition, part of the multi-story winery building can be seen across the field to your left about 1.5 miles along, just before you go under the lines of the electrical towers. It is on private property, however. The park also contains one of California's largest and oldest stands of native western sycamore trees.*

All too soon the bike path ends at the park's main entrance. Exit the park, going left onto Wetmore Road, and retrace your route back to Pleasanton, following the road right as it becomes Holmes, going left on Vallecitos and right on Vineyard.

In Pleasanton, Vineyard goes left on Bernal and then continues to the right. After it becomes Ray Street, you will have rejoined the main route of the ride.

Main route continues: Ray Street brings you back to Main where you turn left. Here is the **Pleasanton Hotel**, rebuilt after the original establishment burned in 1898. Although no longer offering rooms, this attractive building houses an excellent restaurant. Across the street is the Pleasanton Cheese Factory, a popular destination of bicyclists who come here for the large deli sandwiches.

To complete your ride, continue on Main Street over Arroyo del Valle. Just past Stanley Boulevard, use the sidewalk bike path to cross the railroad tracks and ride down to the frontage road paralleling Santa Rita Road, the extension of Main Street. In .75 miles, at the stop sign after Nevis Street, go left on Black and cross Santa Rita at the traffic light. This brings you back to Amador Valley Park, where you started your tour of this growing city that still treasures its small town roots.

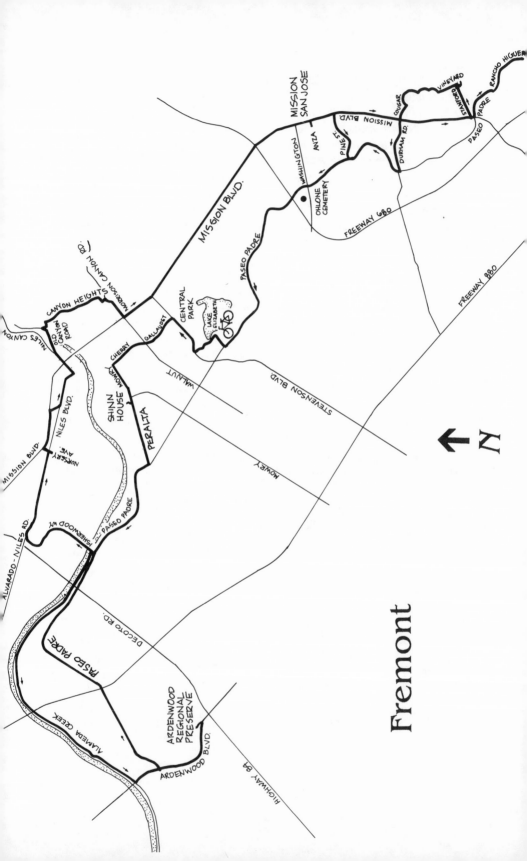

Fremont

Distance: 18 miles with 7 and 11 mile optional side trips

Rating: The main route is **moderate**, with some rolling hills and traffic to contend with. The 7 mile side trip to Stanford/Weibel Winery is rated **moderately strenuous**, while the longer optional route along the Alameda Creek Trail is **easy**. This area can be hot in the summer, and there is little shade. The best time for riding is while the hills are green in winter and spring.

Highlights: Although Fremont is one of the more recently incorporated cities in the area, its origins date back to mission days. This varied tour offers glimpses into many aspects of the town's colorful past, and includes sites from the Spanish period through the days of the silent movie industry. You may also visit an historic farm preserve and 100-year-old winery.

Begin your ride in Central Park on Paseo Padre Parkway. In the park are many of the city's municipal facilities, including a library, community center, civic center, and a recreational area surrounding Lake Elizabeth. There is even a 2 mile bike path around the lake. (Restrooms can also be found in several locations.) The City of Fremont was created in 1956, incorporating as districts the former towns of Niles, Centerville, Mission San Jose, Irvington and Warm Springs.

Pick up the bike path off Sailway Drive near the boat launching area at the lake, going left toward the Civic Center, a dramatic concrete edifice facing Stevenson Boulevard. As you reach the west end of the lake, look for the paved path on the left just past the Civic Center. This takes you to Stevenson, where you go right. In half a mile, make a left turn at Gallaudet Drive, which becomes Cherry Lane after crossing Walnut. At busy Mowry Avenue, go left.

When Mowry angles left, stay to the right, moving onto Peralta Boulevard (Highway 84). Here you take the first right on Sidney, and then immediately go right again and left into the driveway. Although the sign here says "Youth and Family Counseling Services," you have come to view **Shinn Historical Park**.

The small white private residence you see first is the cottage built by Captain William Sim around 1848 of lumber salvaged from ships abandoned in San Francisco Bay. It was purchased by pioneer nursery-

Shinn House

man James Shinn when he and his wife Lucy first came to California
from Texas in 1856. It has since been moved here from its original
location along Alameda Creek.

Beyond the cottage is the Shinn House, a stylish redwood Victorian
ranch home built by the Shinns in 1876. Shinn was noted for his
ornamental plants and fruit and nut trees, some newly introduced from
Japan. The house contains late nineteenth century furnishings, including some memorabilia of the Shinn family.

Also on the property are a foreman's house from about 1910 (now
the counseling center), a barn, and formal gardens containing a number
of Shinn's specimen trees from his early ranch and nursery business.
Although the grounds are open daily from dawn to 10:00 pm, house
tours are given only on the first Wednesday and third Sunday each
month from 1:00 to 3:00 pm, or at special Christmas and spring weekend open houses. Bicycles are not allowed in the park, but you may
lock them just inside the fence.

Leaving the park, return to Peralta, and go right. In less than a mile,
a right turn will take you onto Paseo Padre, where you will have a bike
lane. After 1.5 miles, as the road draws close to Alameda Creek, turn
right at Isherwood Way.

If you are doing the optional easy route to Ardenwood Historic
Farm, here is where you will get on the Alameda Creek bike path. If
you are riding directly to Niles, cross over the creek on Isherwood.

Optional side trip: *Instead of crossing the creek, go right, around the gate, and down the gravel path, turning left on the paved trail going under the bridge. The* **Alameda Creek Regional Trail** *is a paved biking/hiking trail which follows the flood control channel from Niles Canyon to San Francisco Bay, a distance of 12 miles.*

Riding here is tranquil, offering an escape from city traffic and an opportunity to watch the waterfowl that make their home along the creek. You will follow this level trail for 4.3 miles, going under several overpasses. (Water and pit toilets are located in a small park about halfway.) To exit onto Ardenwood/Newark Boulevard, go beneath the overpass at the 7.25 mile marking on the pavement, turning left on the gravel road leading to the street. Here you will have to share the road with fast-moving traffic as you ride right, toward Ardenwood Farm.

The entrance to **Ardenwood Regional Preserve** *is just over a mile away, on the left, after an overpass and just before the entrance to Highway 84. From the distance you can see the grove of eucalyptus and other trees which cover much of the farm, now nearly surrounded by residential subdivisions.*

In the late 1800's George Patterson built Ardenwood into one of the most prosperous farms in the Bay Area. Today only a small portion of Patterson's property remains as part of the farm, the rest sold off for development of tract homes and industrial parks. Visitors can tour this re-creation of a working farm with its acres of crops, walnut orchard, eucalyptus grove, farm animals, and restored antique farm machinery, all designed to give a living picture of farm life in the period between 1870 and 1920.

Ride the half mile to the admissions gate located in the railroad station. (Restrooms are available here.) Bicycles are not allowed past this point, so be sure to bring a lock. You'll want to allow plenty of time for your visit, as there is much to see.

The centerpiece of the park is the stately **Patterson House**. *The rear section was built in 1856, while the large Queen Anne front section was added around 1883 after Patterson's marriage to Clara Hawley. Three generations of Pattersons have lived here. The house contains original family furnishings and is open for tours. Also on the property are barns, animal pens, horse corrals, a blacksmith shop, pool house, gazebo, picnic grounds, and food service.*

The park is open Thursday to Sunday, April through November, from 10:00 am to 4:00 pm, with special Christmas tours in December. It is closed January through March. The admission fee includes house tours, haywagon and railway rides, and special programs and demonstrations. For further information, call 415-796-0663.

Patterson House

After exploring the park, retrace your route on Ardenwood Boulevard less than a mile to Paseo Padre Parkway, where you go right. There is some traffic here, but the street is wide and eventually has a bike lane. You will also have two overpasses. Follow Paseo Padre 3.5 miles to Isherwood Way, turning left to cross over Alameda Creek

Or, if you prefer, you may go back the way you came along the Creek Trail, which will add one mile to your return route. To exit at Isherwood, go beneath the underpass, and right on the gravel section to the bridge over the creek.

Main route continues: Follow Isherwood Way over Alameda Creek. Picnic tables, water, and pit toilets are located on the other side beyond the parking lot. The trail there along the creek is unpaved and used for horseback riding.

Soon Isherwood becomes Quarry Lakes Road as it turns left and heads through open fields and farm lands. At the end of Quarry Lakes, go right on Osprey, and then right onto Alvarado-Niles Road toward the Niles District of Fremont.

In 1.25 miles, you will come to the Mission Adobe Nursery, originally known as the California Nursery Company. Founded in 1865 by John Rock, it was moved to Niles in 1886. It was owned by the Roeding family from 1917 to the early 1970's, and played a major role in the development of the fruit industry in California.

Turn right into the driveway, and ride through the parking lot behind the nursery. There you will find, nearly hidden in the eucalyptus, a small adobe. Built about 1845, probably for the use of overseers and workmen, this was part of Rancho Arroyo de la Alameda granted to Jose de Jesus Vallejo in 1842. Vallejo, elder brother of General Mariano Vallejo, was the first administrator of the secularized Mission San Jose and owned 17,000 acres of former mission land. Today, the adobe is owned by the City of Fremont and available for rental.

Leaving the nursery, cross Niles Boulevard, and take Nursery Avenue straight ahead to Mission Boulevard. Turn to the right, and soon you will see an old railroad station. This 1904 Southern Pacific depot has been moved here from its original location and restored as a museum. It is open the first Saturday of the month from 10:00 am to 2:00 pm.

At the next corner, turn right at the Sullivan Underpass. The road is very narrow here, so you may want to use the sidewalk. At Niles Boulevard, go left into the oldest part of Niles.

Although the town of **Niles**, originally called Vallejo Mills, grew up around Vallejo's flour mills, its real development was associated with the coming of the railroad in 1869. Renamed for state supreme court judge and railroad official Addison Niles, the town became an important rail center for both the Central Pacific and Western Pacific (the reason you cross so many railroad tracks on this tour). But Niles' greatest claim to fame comes from its brief heyday as a movie-making center during the silent film era.

In 1912 Chicago producer George Spoor and his partner "Bronco Billy" Anderson brought their Essenay Film Company to Niles. During the next few years the streets of Niles and the hills of Niles Canyon were used as the setting for nearly 400 one-reel westerns, all starring Bronco Billy. The most famous movie made here, however, was Charlie Chaplin's *The Tramp* in 1915, the last of five he filmed during his three-month stay in Niles. In 1916 the company moved to southern California, and the excitement was over.

Niles today looks much the same as it did then, except main street stores are now filled with antique shops. Nothing remains of the block-long Essenay studio, located at Niles Boulevard between G and F Streets. It was razed in 1933, leaving only a market and parking lot to mark its location. However, several of the small cottages built by the studio to house its staff are still to be found behind the site on 2nd Street, one block from Niles Boulevard.

Follow Niles Boulevard as it leaves downtown, turns left and crosses Mission Boulevard. On the left after the intersection is Vallejo Mill Historical Park, site of Vallejo's flour mills, the first in the area. All that remain today are the ruins of the stone foundation.

You are now riding on Niles Canyon Road, a popular cycling route to Sunol, despite the fast-moving traffic. From Niles Canyon Road, take the first right onto Old Canyon Road. As you cross Alameda Creek, you can see beautiful Niles Canyon ahead of you, the location of many Bronco Billy westerns. You will also pass the beginning of the Alameda Creek Regional Trail. At the first opportunity, turn right on Clarke Drive to Canyon Heights Drive. Go right, and follow Canyon Heights to Maar Avenue. Jog right and left back onto Canyon Heights. At Morrison Canyon Road, turn right and then left at Mission Boulevard.

Ride south on Mission Boulevard for just over 3 miles. You will have a bike lane most of the way and a gradual uphill as you head toward Mission San Jose. Amid all the newer homes and shopping centers, you can still see an occasional farmhouse, barn and water tank, from the area's agricultural past. You may wonder how long it will be before these properties, too, succumb to Fremont's rapid growth.

Shortly before the mission, you will pass the old Beard estate on the right, hidden behind ivy-covered walls and towering palms. Palmdale, built on former mission land, is now the home of the Sisters of the Holy Family, an order begun in San Francisco in 1872.

On the left is **Mission San Jose**, founded by Father Lasuen in 1797. Although conversion of the native Indians went slowly at first, eventually this mission was responsible for over 6700 neophytes. It was also noted for excellence in music and boasted a 30-piece Indian orchestra, organized by Father Duran, who served at the mission from 1806 to 1833. At one time this was probably the most productive and prosperous of all the missions.

A section of an 1809 monastery wing remains and contains an interesting museum, worthy of a visit. It is open daily from 10:00 am to 5:00 pm. The main church, however, was destroyed by the earthquake of 1868, one of the largest in California's recorded history. A wooden church called St. Joseph's was built the next year on the site and used until 1965, when a new St. Joseph's was completed nearby. The old building was later sold to an Episcopalian congregation and moved to San Mateo to make way for the construction of a replica of the original mission church. The large structure you see today is an historically accurate reconstruction completed in 1985 at a cost of $5 million. The inside has also been beautifully decorated, as befits the mission's status as one of California's richest.

Under the floor of the church are the graves of Robert Livermore and his wife Josefa Higuera, as well as other members of his family. Livermore was a wealthy rancher after whom the town of Livermore was named. It was long thought that the family had been buried at Mission San Jose, but the exact location was not known. The site was discovered as a result of the archeological dig prior to the restoration of the mission. Being among the most prominent citizens of the area, the family had been awarded the honor of interment in the mission itself, but the graves were apparently hidden by rubble after the 1868 earthquake.

The tombstones of many of the county's early pioneers can be found by exploring the cemetery next door. Don Vallejo's elegant hacienda was once located across the street from the mission church.

Continue south on Mission Boulevard for a view of the town which grew up around the mission. This community was the center of social life during the time of the Californios and a boisterous provision center for the Forty-Niners heading to the southern mines during the Gold Rush.

The bed and breakfast inn next to the mission was once the Washington Hotel, built in 1856. (The house with the tower is new.) Note the red brick building on the right, at #43363, originally the Ehrman General Store and later the Wells Fargo office. It was built in 1894, replacing an old adobe store on the site. Two doors down the street is an old saloon, now a flower shop.

Turn right at Anza Street to see #152, a beautifully restored Victorian, built in 1890 as the rectory for the old St. Joseph's Church. It was moved to its present location in 1979 to make room for the mission reconstruction.

St. Joseph's Rectory

Return to Mission Boulevard, and go right. In the next block is the Old School, at #43551, a complex of shops and offices in a 1913 school building. This structure has also been used as Fremont's City Hall and as classrooms for Ohlone College, the community college located across the street and up the hill on what was once the old mission vineyards.

From here you may either head back to Central Park or continue on to the Warm Springs District and the Stanford/Weibel Winery. To return to your starting point, stay on Mission for 2 blocks, turning right on Pine Street. When you reach Paseo Padre Parkway at the bottom of a downhill, go right.

Optional side trip: The route south is moderately hilly, and traffic may be heavy along Mission Boulevard. But you are compensated by fine views of Mission Peak and the surrounding hills.

Ride on Mission for 2 miles until you see signs pointing to Mission Peak Regional Preserve and Weibel Winery. Continue one very short block beyond (you will stop at the winery on your return), turning left on Paseo Padre Parkway.

Go left again in half a mile when you reach Rancho Higuera Road. At the next corner you will find what is thought to be the largest syca- more tree in the state, discovered when the surrounding houses were being built.

Continue along Rancho Higuera for a short climb. As you reach the top you will see the small white Galindo-Higuera Adobe sitting in isolation on the hill to the left. Although the adobe is open infrequently (usually the third Saturday afternoon of the month during the summer), a small display at the bottom of the hill gives the history of the building and its restoration.

The adobe was located on Rancho de Agua Caliente, granted to Fulgencio Higuera in 1839. It was probably built about 1842 by Juan Crisostoma Galindo, who purchased part of the Higuera rancho. Largely in ruins by the 1960's, in 1978 it was carefully restored to its former appearance and furnished with replicas of the period. It is not much to look at when contrasted with the large new homes across the street, but it is an excellent example of the rustic lifestyle of Mexican California.

*Return downhill to Paseo Padre, turning right. When you reach Mission Boulevard, go right and immediately right again onto Stanford Avenue. This eucalyptus-lined street will take you to the **Weibel Winery** and Champagne Vineyards.*

In 1776 the explorer De Anza named the creek here Agua Caliente for the warm springs which the Indians had long frequented. This was a fashionable resort area from 1850 until the earthquake of 1868 de- stroyed the buildings. Wealthy vacationers, as well as invalids, came from all over to enjoy the benefits of the hot sulphur water.

In 1869 all this property was acquired by Leland Stanford, railroad builder, United States Senator and founder of Stanford University. With his brother Josiah, he planted the vineyards and founded the winery which was among the earliest to produce California fine wines. Weibel Winery still uses two of the old Stanford brick buildings located beyond the tasting room, which is open daily from 10:00 am to 5:00 pm. (Restrooms are available here.)

From the winery, continue up Stanford a very short distance to the roadway on the right leading to Hidden Valley. There you will see the building constructed as a hotel in 1869 by A. A. Cohen of Alameda. It was never used for that purpose, however, instead becoming the home of Josiah Stanford, and later his son, also named Josiah. Now a restaurant and bar, it has also been used as a convent and brothel (although not at the same time).

Return to Stanford Avenue, crossing to Vineyard Avenue, which takes you past many of the new, large homes being built in this area. Go right at Antelope Drive for a short steep uphill. Make right turns at Boar Circle, Cougar Circle, and Cougar Drive, where a fast downhill brings you to Mission Boulevard. Crossing Mission, the road becomes Durham Road. In a mile you will come back to Paseo Padre once again, where you go right up the hill. In less than a mile, Paseo Padre crosses Pine, and you will have rejoined the main route.

Main route continues: Continuing on Paseo Padre past Pine, you will cross Washington Boulevard in just over half a mile. To the left, beyond the trees, is the Ohlone Cemetery, where 4000 Indians who built and worked at Mission San Jose are buried. This is considered sacred ground and trespassing is forbidden. There is little to see here but a sign declaring this to be an American Indian Historic Site, a monument to the decimation of the tribe after the coming of the Spanish.

The Ohlones lived a comfortable life before the mission was established, with a plentiful supply of acorns, seeds, fruits, game, fish and shellfish. Their huts were constructed of bent willows covered with tule rushes, and they wove extraordinarily fine baskets. The culture of these generous and hospitable people was mostly destroyed after they were taken from their villages to live and work at the mission.

From here it is 2.5 miles back to Central Park, the conclusion of your tour of Fremont, one of the East Bay's most historically diverse regions.

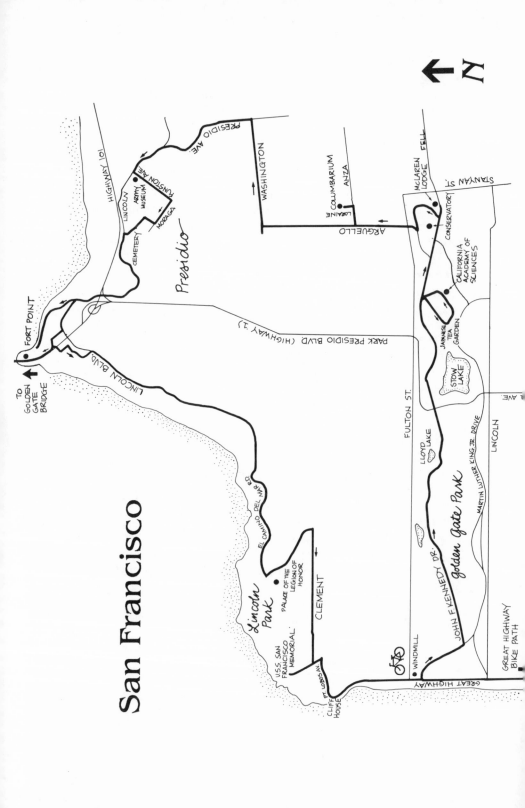

San Francisco

San Francisco

Distance: 21 miles

Rating: The route is rated **moderately strenuous** for numerous short climbs and busy city traffic, although it does avoid the steepest hills and worst congestion of San Francisco. And some parts of the ride are actually quite flat and easy, including segments that go through Golden Gate Park and across the Bridge. Be prepared for cool temperatures if the city is covered with fog, common in San Francisco, especially during the summer months.

Highlights: This exciting ride traces San Francisco's rich heritage from its early days as a barren military outpost through its more recent development as one of the nation's most beautiful cities. Along the way, you will experience some of its best-known attractions—Golden Gate Park, the Presidio, and Golden Gate Bridge.

The history of San Francisco dates back to 1776 when the Spanish chose it as the location for a military outpost or presidio, and Franciscan padres established Mission Dolores. For the next quarter century, the only inhabitants were Spanish soldiers and their families, padres and mission Indians. Although the soldiers suffered from boredom and minimal rations, the Indians fared much worse. Herded into the mission compound, they succumbed in great numbers to diseases introduced by the Spanish intruder.

After the turn of the century, the harbor at Yerba Buena, as the settlement was then known, began to see increased ship traffic from whalers and Russian sea otter hunters. In 1822 William Richardson arrived by whaling ship, married the eldest daughter of the commander of the Presidio (by then under Mexican control), and became the first non-Spanish white settler of what would eventually become the city of San Francisco.

American settlers followed, and in 1846, the United States seized control of California. At that time Yerba Buena was still a tiny settlement of only a few hundred people. The Gold Rush changed all that, however. Overnight the sleepy little town turned into a bustling, noisy, dirty tent city. The harbor was crowded with ships, many abandoned as their crews headed for the gold fields. Fortune hunters swarmed into the city from all over the world, swelling the population to 100,000.

As the supply of gold ran out, the city's importance suddenly declined and its numbers dwindled. But San Francisco was not destined for obscurity. It became headquarters for the operations of the Comstock silver mines in Virginia City, Nevada, and for the transcontinental railroad, completed in 1869. Despite periods of boom and bust, the city grew; by 1900 it had over 300,000 inhabitants.

This was a time when millionaires and multi-millionaires vied with each other to see who could spend their money in the most ostentatious ways. Fantastic mansions were built by Crocker, Flood, Hopkins, and Stanford on Nob Hill. A wonderful assortment of Victorian homes was constructed by the less affluent in other parts of the city.

Then the most famous event in San Francisco's history occurred. On April 18, 1906, a major earthquake shook the city. The fire that ensued destroyed dwellings of the wealthy and poor alike, leaving more than 200,000 homeless. San Francisco was quickly rebuilt, however, and since that time has gradually developed into one of America's most cosmopolitan and accessible cities.

Begin your tour of "everybody's favorite city" at Ocean Beach on the Great Highway, located at the west end of Golden Gate Park, between Fulton Street and Lincoln Way. Parking is available along the Esplanade. Restrooms can be found at several locations within the park.

Golden Gate Park is one of the largest man-made parks in the world. In 1870, when the site for the 1017 acre park was selected, this area was on the outskirts of town and consisted mostly of sand dunes. The initial park design was created by William Hammond Hall, the park's first superintendent. Hall applied innovative sand reclamation techniques and began planting trees.

The name most people associate with the park, however, is that of John McLaren, a Scottish landscape gardener who was appointed superintendent in 1887. Golden Gate Park became the love of his life, and he devoted the next 55 years to its development. Under his guidance, thousands of trees were planted (mostly Monterey cypress, Monterey pine, and eucalyptus), as well as numerous varieties of rhododendron. The completed park remains a monument to McLaren's skill in landscape design and his love of nature.

Enter the park on John F. Kennedy Drive near Fulton Street, between the windmill and Beach Chalet. The Dutch Windmill was built in 1902 to pump the thousands of gallons of water needed to irrigate the plantings in the park. After electric pumps were installed in the 1920's, the windmill fell into disrepair until renovated in 1981. The Queen Wilhelmina Garden here is especially beautiful when the tulips bloom in the spring. A second windmill, built in 1905, is located at the south corner of the park and has not been restored.

The Beach Chalet, on the Great Highway, is a Spanish Revival style building, which opened as a municipal restaurant in 1925. It was the last work of the great architect Willis Polk. In the process of being restored, it will soon open again as a bar and restaurant.

Since most of the attractions in the park are located on the eastern side, this end is more peaceful and less traveled. As you ride along enjoying the lush greenery, try to imagine what this area looked like before 1870 when it consisted of sand dunes, or just after the 1906 earthquake when thousands of refugee shacks were erected in the park for those who had lost their homes.

At the first stop sign, stay on Kennedy Drive as it turns left. (Martin Luther King Jr. Drive goes straight ahead.) You will have gentle uphill bicycling for about 2 miles.

Soon you will pass the Buffalo Paddock, Rhododendron Island (where the road divides) and Spreckels Lake. In about .75 miles you will come to Lloyd Lake on your left. You are likely to hear and see the "rapids" feeding the tiny lake first. Stop a moment and look at the structure across the pond. Called "Portals of the Past," this doorway is all that was left of the A. N. Towne residence located on Nob Hill after the 1906 fire. (If you are bicycling on a Sunday, you will be happy to find that JFK Drive is closed to automobile traffic after this point.)

In less than a mile further along, go right to reach the museums. You will be greeted by a statue of Padre Junipero Serra, founder of the California missions, one of many sculptures located here. The large depression beyond is the Music Concourse. At the far end stands the Spreckels Temple of Music, an ornate band shell constructed in 1900. It is the home of the Golden Gate Park Band, the oldest, continuously operating municipal band in the country. Free music programs of all kinds are regularly held here.

The Concourse was the site of the 1894 Midwinter International Exposition. A 210-foot high Tower of Electricity was a major feature of that 200 acre fair, which included over 100 temporary buildings, as well as a lively midway. When the fair closed, only the Japanese Village was preserved, later to become the Japanese Tea Garden.

Follow the one-way street right to the M. H. de Young Memorial Museum, which houses a major collection of western art from ancient times to the 20th century. It is open Wednesday through Sunday, 10:00 am to 5:00 pm. There is an admission fee, which also covers the Asian Art Museum next door. The museums are free on the first Wednesday of the month.

The **Japanese Tea Garden** beyond is the oldest Japanese-style garden in the United States. Tea and cookies are served in the pavilion overlooking the garden. Open daily, there is an admission charge, except on the first Wednesday of the month and major holidays.

To cross to the other side of the concourse, walk your bike behind the Music Temple (restrooms can be found here). Ride left on the one-way by the California Academy of Sciences, which includes Morrison Planetarium and Steinhart Aquarium. The Academy is open daily from 10:00 am to 5:00 pm. It, too, is free the first Wednesday of the month.

Return to JFK Drive, and go right a short distance to the **Conservatory of Flowers**, the oldest remaining building in Golden Gate Park. This beautiful Victorian crystal palace is a replica of one in Kew Gardens, London. Prefabricated and shipped around the Horn, it was initially intended for the James Lick estate in Santa Clara. After Lick's death in 1876, it was purchased by the city and installed here two years later. The Conservatory is open every day.

Conservatory of Flowers

The Richardsonian Romanesque building a short distance past the Conservatory is McLaren Lodge. To see it, turn left at the stop sign, walking your bike on the pedestrian crosswalk. This building served as John McLaren's home and office from 1896 until his death in 1943 at age 93. Now it houses the San Francisco Parks Department. Stanyan Street just beyond marks the edge of the main part of the park. Turn around here, riding to the next corner, where you go right up one-way

Conservatory Drive. At the top of the rise, at the stop sign, make a right turn downhill to exit the park onto Arguello Street, heading into the busy city.

The ride down Arguello may involve some traffic, but there is usually room for both cars and bicycles. To view one of the lesser known buildings of San Francisco, turn right on Anza in several blocks. The second left onto Loraine Court brings you to the Neptune Society **Columbarium**, a repository for urns containing cremated ashes. This elegant neoclassic, green-domed structure, erected in 1898 for the Independent Order of Odd Fellows, is as lovely inside as out, with stained glass windows, marble flooring, and ceiling mosaics. It is open to the public Tuesday through Saturday, 9:00 am to 1:00 pm, and is definitely worth a visit.

Leaving the columbarium, retrace your route and continue on Arguello. In one block you will cross busy Geary Boulevard, which in the 1860's was a private four-mile toll road leading to oceanside Cliff House. The domed Temple Emanu-El, built in 1926, is ahead.

Shortly after the temple and before the steep uphill, a left turn brings you into Presidio Terrace, a collection of large mansions dating from the early 1900's. Perhaps the most unusual is #30, immediately on the left, an immense Hansel and Gretel cottage dating from 1909. After admiring the homes, cross Arguello, riding straight ahead on Washington. This uphill route takes you through the residential area known as Presidio Heights and by many of San Francisco's finest homes from the early part of the century. The 1902 Koshland Mansion (#3800) at the intersection with Maple is particularly impressive.

When you reach Presidio Avenue in another half mile, go left. Soon you will enter the **Presidio of San Francisco**, a military base for over 200 years. In 1776 Juan Bautista de Anza, commander of the first group of Spanish settlers, chose this site for a military post and built a walled camp on the rocky promontory. After Mexico won its independence from Spain, Mexican soldiers were garrisoned here until the United States took possession in 1846.

The Presidio is situated on the northernmost point of the San Francisco peninsula, and originally its sandy, rocky hills were almost bare of vegetation. The Spainards considered this a hardship post because of the wind, fog, and scarcity of trees and water. Eucalyptus and pine trees were planted in the 1880's, and today, it is one of San Francisco's prettiest spots. Scheduled to be closed as a military base, the Presidio will become part of the Golden Gate National Recreation Area; it is not yet known how the buildings will be used.

Immediately as you enter the Presidio grounds, you begin a long downhill. Be careful here, as the road is narrow, although traffic is not heavy. On the way down, you will have a fine view of the Palace of Fine Arts below, built for the 1915 Panama-Pacific Exposition, and the bay beyond.

At the bottom of the hill, traffic increases as Lombard Street joins from the right at the stop sign. Soon you are on busy Lincoln Boulevard. When you reach Funston Avenue, turn left, following the 49-Mile Scenic Drive sign, and stop at the **Presidio Army Museum** on the corner.

Dating from 1857, this building is the oldest structure on the post built by the United States Army. Used as a hospital and dispensary for over 100 years, it is now a museum containing exhibits and dioramas of the Presidio's colorful past. It is open free to the public, Tuesday through Sunday between 10:00 am and 4:00 pm. Detailed maps of the Presidio grounds are also available here. Be sure to examine the two small shacks behind the museum. These were built to house refugees in Golden Gate Park after the 1906 earthquake.

From the museum, continue along Funston to see a fine collection of early Victorian style homes. Some were constructed as early as 1862 for officers and are used for the same purpose today. Follow the road right onto Moraga Avenue. The Officers Club on the left is built around a section of adobe wall from the original Spanish headquarters, probably the first building erected in San Francisco.

In two blocks make a right onto Montgomery Street. The row of Georgian style red brick barracks, dating from 1895, comprises the first permanent barracks built by the Army here. At Sheridan (following the 49-Mile Drive sign), a left turn will bring you back to Lincoln Boulevard, where you go left by the National Cemetery. In use since 1852, it contains over 24,000 graves, including those for Colonel Edwin Baker, General Frederick Funston, and General Hunter Ligget, as well as Pauline Fryer, an actress and Union spy, and "Two Bits," an Indian scout for the Army.

Continue on Lincoln Boulevard for less than a mile. Just after the stop sign, as Lincoln starts to climb left to the Golden Gate Bridge, angle right on the narrow downhill road leading to **Fort Point**, built in 1861 to guard the harbor of San Francisco. As you ride along the water, be aware that waves sometimes wash over the road! Ahead is the massive red brick fort situated under a span of the Golden Gate Bridge.

The strategic significance of this location has been recognized since the Spanish erected an adobe fort here in the late 18th century. The United States Army replaced the ruins of that building with the impressive fortress you see today. Fort Point was designed to mount 126 cannon with a range of up to two miles and to house 600 soldiers. Three interesting granite spiral staircases open onto the courtyard, and a lighthouse, built in 1864, sits on top of one of them. The walls average 5 to 12 feet in thickness.

The fort, officially named Fort Winfield Scott, is administered by the National Park Service and is open free to the public daily from 10:00 am to 5:00 pm. You can wander through its three tiers on your own or join a ranger-led tour. Be sure to climb to the roof for fine views of the ocean and bay.

Fort Point

Return up the steep road, going right, back onto Lincoln Boulevard. To reach the **Golden Gate Bridge**, make a right turn into the View Area parking lot just before the Highway 101 underpass.

In the View Area is a statue of Joseph B. Straus, chief engineer of the bridge. There is also a cross section of bridge cable and a colorful flower garden. This is a popular picture-taking spot for San Francisco's many tourists. Restrooms are located nearby.

To begin your ride across the bridge, bicycle up the slight incline by the visitor center. At the beginning of the bridge, a sign will inform you where to ride. On weekdays you will use the sidewalk on the bay (east) side of the bridge. On weekends you will be directed to a path under the bridge to reach the ocean (west) side.

The Golden Gate Bridge was completed in 1937 to connect San Francisco and Marin Counties. Its two towers rise 746 feet above the water. Enjoy your thrilling 2 mile ride across this much beloved landmark and the splendid views it offers of the Marin Headlands ahead, and Angel Island, Alcatraz and San Francisco on your right.

At the end of the bridge on the bay side is popular Vista Point (restrooms are also located here). If you are riding on the ocean side and want to reach this point, you will have to use the pedestrian underpass at the end of the bridge. This necessitates carrying your bike down and up the stairs.

When you have taken in the views of the city, bridge, and Fort Baker below, retrace your route and enjoy an exhilarating ride back across the bridge to the View Area on the San Francisco side. (Or, if you want to add more miles, you may connect with the Marin Headlands route.)

From the View Area, ride right on the road that goes under the bridge approach, following the bike route markings. Turn left and then right onto Merchant Road, toward Golden Gate NRA. As you ride up the hill to rejoin Lincoln Boulevard, you will pass a reinforced concrete battery on your right. This was one of several military fortifications built at the turn of the century to protect the city's harbor.

At Lincoln, make a right turn. You will have the ocean on your right and the Presidio grounds to your left. Traffic is frequently heavy here, and the shoulder is often narrow. After a short climb, you will have a mile-long downhill. Two parking areas along the way provide places to stop and again appreciate views of the bridge and Marin Headlands.

As the road levels out, Lincoln becomes El Camino del Mar Road and passes some fine San Francisco homes. Continue to follow the 49-Mile Scenic Drive signs, which, after a half-mile strenuous climb, direct you left onto Legion of Honor Drive.

Here is the California **Palace of the Legion of Honor**, located in Lincoln Park. This splendid art museum, built by a donation from Adolph and Alma Spreckels, was dedicated in 1924 to the "youth of our land who died to make men free" during World War I. It is a replica of the Palace of Legion of Honor in Paris. The museum is open Wednesday to Sunday from 10:00 am to 5:00 pm. There is an admission fee except on Saturday morning and the first Wednesday of the month. The views of the Golden Gate Bridge and Marin Headlands from the plaza in front of the museum are breathtaking.

Nearby is the Lincoln Park Municipal Golf Course. This was the location of Golden Gate Cemetery from 1868 to 1900, when it was decided no longer to allow interment within the city limits. In 1909, the cemetery was turned into a park, and many of the graves were left undisturbed and unmarked.

A downhill past the museum brings you to Clement, where you go right. Clement has more climbing and, after passing the Veterans

Administration Medical Center, becomes Seal Rock Drive. At its end, a right turn on El Camino Del Mar brings you to a large parking lot and the USS San Francisco Memorial. This is the actual bridge of the USS San Francisco, which lost 107 members of its crew in the Battle of Guadalcanal in 1942. From here you will also have an excellent view of the Point Bonita Lighthouse across the Golden Gate.

To continue your ride, turn around, taking the first right on Point Lobos Avenue. This is a fast downhill which soon becomes the Great Highway and takes you by Cliff House. Traffic is often congested at this popular tourist attraction, so be sure to use caution.

The original 1863 **Cliff House** was purchased by Adolph Sutro in 1882. When that building burned in 1894, he rebuilt it as a fantastic Victorian hotel and added its famous baths. The Sutro Baths had five saltwater pools of different temperatures and one freshwater plunge.

Sutro, who had made his fortune as an engineer in the Comstock silver mines, served San Francisco as mayor, donated land for the University of California medical school, gained protection for the sea lions that occupied Seal Rocks, and left his fine collection of books and Egyptian art to the public. He also developed a fabulous garden at his estate, Sutro Heights, on the bluff across from Cliff House. Today, his estate is a city park. The imaginative 1894 Cliff House was destroyed by fire in 1907 and replaced by the present utilitarian building, which has been remodeled several times. The Baths burned in 1966, leaving only ruins to be seen today.

Walk down a flight of stairs to the view area for dramatic vistas of the coast and to watch the sea lions offshore on Seal Rocks. On this level also is the National Park Service Visitor Center, which houses historic photographs of earlier Cliff Houses and the Sutro Baths. Other attractions here include the present-day Cliff House restaurant.

From Cliff House, it is only a short distance back to your starting point at the beach. If you want to add a flat, pleasant ride along the ocean, you can do a few more miles on the Great Highway bike path. To reach the path, continue to the far end of the parking area. There, at the signal that regulates traffic on Lincoln Way, cross the highway to pick up the bike path on the other side. This will take you 2 miles to Sloat Boulevard, where the path ends. On your return, if the ocean breezes have developed into an uncomfortably strong headwind, you may want to ride on one of the inland streets, such as 47th.

This completes your ride of San Francisco. With its rich historical background, spectacular sweeping views, and aura of sophistication, it is easy to understand why this enchanting city is one of the best-loved in the world.

Half Moon Bay

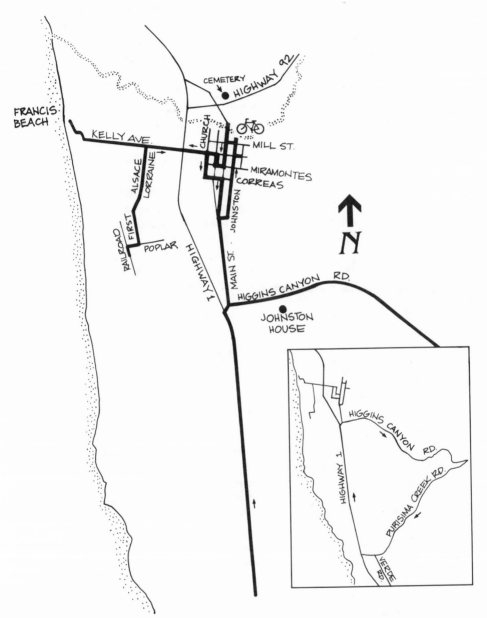

Half Moon Bay

Distance: 7 miles with 11 mile optional side trip

Rating: The shorter ride is flat and **easy**, taking place on quiet streets with light to moderate traffic. The optional side trip, however, is **strenuous**. It includes a steep uphill on a narrow winding road and the possibility of a coastal headwind on the return segment. Riding in Half Moon Bay is most pleasant during the off season, without the beach goers. Also, be sure to avoid the third weekend in October, the date of the annual Pumpkin Festival, when the town is crowded with tourists.

Highlights: Despite its proximity to Bay Area urban centers and the desirability of its beaches, Half Moon Bay has retained much of its small farming town charm and simplicity. The tour includes visits to sites which exemplify the town's rural history, as well as an excursion to the beach. The optional route through inland canyons takes you by old ranch buildings, and offers the chance to enjoy peaceful country roads and ocean vistas.

The history of Half Moon Bay can be traced to Gaspar de Portola, who camped here on his expedition from Mexico in 1769 in search of the bay at Monterey. He discovered instead San Francisco Bay, first sighted from Sweeney Ridge. At that time, this was the land of the Costanoan Indians, who lived near Pilarcitos Creek. When Mission Dolores was founded in San Francisco in 1776, the area became the mission grazing land. The Indians were sent to work at the San Pedro mission ranch, which supplied food for the mission and presidio.

With the secularization of the mission system after Mexico achieved its independence from Spain, the pastures were divided into ranchos. The southern part of Rancho El Corral de Tierra (north of Pilarcitos Creek) was granted to Tiburcio Vasquez in 1839. Rancho Arroyo de los Pilarcitos, south of the creek and also known as Rancho San Benito, was granted to Candelario Miramontes in 1841. These two large families with their many children were company and protection for each other, and together constituted the earliest settlers of what was to become the town of Half Moon Bay.

Half Moon Bay's early economy was based on the raising of cattle and sheep. This is still an important activity, although today the main industry is growing flowers, such as chrysanthemums, carnations and roses. The principal vegetable crops are brussels sprouts, artichokes and, of course, pumpkins. Tourism is also a major industry.

Begin your ride at the parking lot located at Johnston and Mill Streets, one block off Main Street. The Miramontes adobe ranch house was originally located here but has long since disappeared.

Go right on Mill and right again on Main, heading north toward Highway 92. Soon you will cross over Pilarcitos Creek, the dividing line between the two land grants. The bridge, constructed of steel-reinforced concrete, was an engineering marvel at the time it was built in 1900. It replaced an earlier wooden wagon bridge, part of the San Mateo-Half Moon Bay Turnpike, a precarious wagon road over the mountains. A toll gate was located several miles up the canyon.

Stop across from the first house on the left, #270. This is known as the Pilarcitos House, and was built by the youngest son of rancho owner Vasquez in 1869. Pablo Vasquez constructed this redwood Greek Revival style home just south of his father's adobe. Its rear annex was added in 1892. The adobe, which was probably the first house built in the area, no longer exists.

The Vasquez descendents continued to be prominent in the community well into the 20th century. The original grantee did not fare so well, however—he was gunned down in a Half Moon Bay saloon in 1863.

Cross back over the bridge. At #326 Main is the charming blue Zaballa house, built in 1859. Zaballa married one of Miramontes' daughters and was owner of the general store and saloon. He also was responsible for the plotting of Half Moon Bay, then called Spanishtown, in 1863.

Half Moon Bay was originally known as San Benito, after the Miramontes rancho. During the 1850's, however, the newly arrived Yankees began calling it Spanishtown. The next 20 years brought rapid growth, with immigration from a variety of European countries, including many Portuguese. By the 1870's, it was decided to rename the town Half Moon Bay, a term that had been used for the entire farming district around the crescent shaped beach. Still, it took about 50 years for the name to become commonly used for the town proper.

Continue down Main Street to the old Mosconi Hotel, dating from 1905. It is now the popular San Benito House and Saloon. As you ride along Main Street, you will see a variety of commercial and residential buildings from the late 19th and early 20th centuries. Most of the old adobe and brick buildings were destroyed by the earthquake of 1906, but many frame structures withstood the shock.

At the corner of Main and Kelly Avenue is Cunha's Country Store, operating in this location since 1924. The building was constructed in 1900 by Joseph Debenedetti, a pioneer merchant. Across the street is **Mac Dutra Park**, a small plaza with picnic tables and restrooms. The recently built brick tower on the corner holds old fire and school bells. On the other side of Main Street is the City Hall, housed in a former bank building.

The false-front structure further down the street on the left, at # 527, is the oldest place of continuous business in town. Built in 1873, it was originally Boitano's General Store and Saloon. Turn right at the next corner onto Miramontes Street and right again on Purissima Street. Dr. Milliken, an early country doctor, had his home and office at #546 on the corner.

Before turning left at Kelly Avenue, the next cross street, look to the right to see the 1928 Dutra Funeral Home, an outstanding example of Art Nouveau architecture. Proceeding down Kelly, you will soon come to Our Lady of the Pillar Catholic Church. The church was built in 1954, but the bronze bell on the front lawn dates from 1867, having been originally located in the chapel at Pilarcitos Cemetery on Highway 92. The stained glass windows in the sanctuary are from an earlier 1883 church building.

Across the street and further down, at #520, is an elegant Eastlake style house built in 1908 by Ben Cunha, a contractor. It is presently called the **Alves House** for the family that lived here after 1923. Converted to retail use, it contains an interesting variety of shops.

Continue along Kelly, crossing Highway 1. At the end of the road is the entrance to the **Francis Beach** section of Half Moon Bay State Beach. You may want to ride into the parking lot, lock your bike and walk the beach for a bit. From here you will have a good view of the four mile crescent of sandy beaches, which gave the town its name. Pillar Point is at the far end. The park has restrooms and camping facilities, including sites for bicyclists, should you plan to stay overnight. For information call 415-726-6238.

Return on Kelly, turning right before Highway 1 on Alsace-Lorraine Avenue, which soon becomes First Street. The new homes here are a sign of Half Moon Bay's expanding population. In about half a mile, just after the road narrows, turn right on Poplar Street. At the next corner, take a left onto Railroad Avenue, a gravel street.

The building before you was once a station for the Ocean Shore Railway, a railroad project originally designed to run along the beach from San Francisco to Santa Cruz. It was completed only as far as Tunitas Glen, but did help hasten the growth of Half Moon Bay. The railroad went out of business in 1920, when the automobile provided a more popular means of transportation. Notice the station's second story dormer, which allowed the stationmaster a clear view of the tracks located along what is presently Railroad Avenue. This 1908 building is now a private residence.

Return the way you came, and at Kelly, turn right, back toward town. The first right after Highway 1 brings you onto Church Street. In 2 blocks go left onto Correas Street. When you reach Main Street again, turn right.

#711 Main, on the left, was the 1875 home of the Debenedettis and was originally located three blocks north. In 1906 Frank Bernardo purchased the building and moved it to this location by rolling it on logs. The house has been remodeled for use as offices.

As you continue down Main, you may wonder about the I.D.E.S. (Irmandade do Divino Espirito Santo) Hall. Erected in 1928 to replace the original wooden building, it houses a Portuguese religious society, the Brotherhood of the Divine Holy Spirit. The colorful Holy Ghost Festival is held here on Pentecost Sunday.

Further down the block on the left are two homes dating from the 1890's, #775 and #779, which have been converted to commercial use. One is now a bed and breakfast inn. On the corner of Metzgar Street, set back from the road at #940, is the old Metzgar house from the 1870's. The Metzgars were an early San Mateo County pioneer family, and their home was built in the unadorned Greek Revival style.

When Main Street ends, turn left onto Higgins Canyon Road. From here you can see the **White House** of Half Moon Bay, the earliest frame home still standing along coastside San Mateo County.

James Johnston was a Forty-Niner from Ohio who came to Half Moon Bay in 1853. With money he had made as a San Francisco saloon keeper and land speculator, he purchased part of the Miramontes' rancho south of town. There he built this comfortable New England style farmhouse for his Spanish wife Petra. At his urging, James' three brothers also came to Half Moon Bay. William's 1854 farm house is located directly across the road.

The Johnston brothers were successful farmers and cattle ranchers for several years, and the beautifully furnished "White House" was the center of social and cultural life for the Half Moon Bay area. But hard times fell on James. His wife and their only daughter both died in 1860. Financial losses forced him to sell much of his land. He died in San Francisco some years later, poor and alone. He is buried in the Half Moon Bay Cemetery on Highway 92, along with other members of his family. His large house sat weatherbeaten and empty for many years. Today it is being restored by the Johnston House Foundation.

At this point you may either retrace your route back into town or continue along Higgins Canyon Road for the optional 11 mile side trip. The latter route is for experienced cyclists only.

Johnston White House

Optional side trip: *About a mile past the Johnston house the narrow road along Arroyo Leon begins to climb. You will have glimpses of some old ranch buildings and views of the ocean as you ride higher. You will also experience a sense of what the area must have been like in former, quieter times. The last uphill mile is very steep (8.5% grade). The mile-long downhill is narrow and winding, but there is little traffic to disturb you. At the bottom of the hill, just after the creek crossing, is Purisima Creek Redwoods Open Space Preserve.*

Purisima Canyon inland was once the site of the longest running logging operation in Peninsula history. From the 1850's to 1920, the Hatch family harvested timber and ran a sawmill near here.

Follow rolling Purisima Creek Road 4 miles back out to Highway 1. Just before the intersection, Verde Road joins from the left, and you will pass a stand of eucalyptus trees. This was the site of the once flourishing town of Purisima. It was a lively place in the 1860's with a hotel, saloon, store, post office, and school, as well as the 17-room Dobbel house, the finest in the area. Today, only the trees remain.

When you reach Highway 1, go right for your 3 mile return to Half Moon Bay. You may encounter headwinds, so be forewarned. As you approach town, you will see the Johnston House on the hill. Turn right at Higgins-Purisima Road and left back onto Main Street to rejoin the main route of the ride.

Main route continues: Ride on Main Street for half a mile, turning right at Monte Vista Lane and left in one block onto Johnston Street. In the next block, at #611, is the former Half Moon Bay Grammar School, built in 1858. When James Johnston's son, also named James, was five years old, there were no English-speaking schools in Spanishtown. So Johnston had a school built near his home on Higgins Road. In 1865 the school was moved to its present location. It was later used as a temperance lodge and is now a private home. Despite some alteration, the look of a one-room schoolhouse remains. The house next door, at #607, is an interesting example of Craftsman bungalow style architecture, typical of California buildings in the 1910's.

Methodist-Episcopal Church

At the intersection of Johnston and Miramontes Streets you will see the Methodist-Episcopal Church. Built in 1872, this is one of the oldest Protestant churches in the county. The attached structure on the left was once the Half Moon Bay station of the Ocean Shore Railroad. Names of early town families of all religious denominations are found in the sidewalk laid around the property in 1911. Half a block further down the street is the former Half Moon Bay jail, at #505 Johnston. This solid concrete building with its barred windows has two cells in the rear. It is now the **Spanishtown Historical Society Museum**.

Turn right on Kelly at the next intersection. On the corner is #751, the old unrestored Simmons House. It was built in 1865 by the town's first undertaker, who was also a carpenter. One block further along, at #505 San Benito, you will come upon a pretty little Queen Anne Victorian dating from 1892. The two-story building behind it with the false front was once a bakery.

Return to Johnston Street, turning right. Soon you will reach your starting point, perhaps wondering how long Half Moon Bay will manage to retain its old-fashioned small town atmosphere in the face of a growing population. This is an issue that concerns its citizens, many of whom actively resist plans for development of the area, hoping to preserve the simplicity and charm you have enjoyed today.

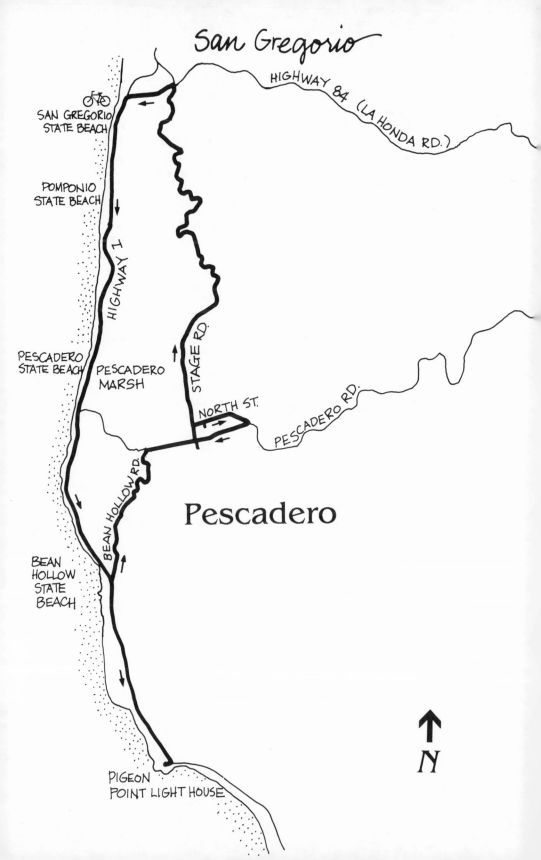

Pescadero

Distance: 28 miles

Rating: This is a **strenuous** ride with several significant hills on
Highway 1 and Stage Road. There is also the possibility of heavy traffic
along the highway, especially on a summer weekend. Be prepared for
morning fog, common on the coast during summer months, even when
warm and sunny inland. The route is planned to take advantage of the
prevailing winds, generally north to south.

Highlights: This tour takes you to the tiny coastal villages of Pescadero and San Gregorio, once major resort areas, and to historic Pigeon
Point Lighthouse. You will ride alongside miles of beaches and pound-
ing surf and on quiet country roads.

Begin your ride at San Gregorio State Beach on Highway 1,
just south of the intersection with Highway 84. There is a charge for
parking here, and pit toilets are available but no water. In fact, there is
no drinking water or food along Highway 1 until Gazos Creek Road, 2.5
miles south of the lighthouse.

Gaspar de Portola and his men camped near San Gregorio Beach in
1769 while traveling overland from San Diego in search of the Bay at
Monterey. After missing Monterey, they went on to discover San
Francisco Bay instead.

From the parking lot, go right onto Highway 1, the beginning of a
dramatic ride along the ocean. Immediately, as you cross San Gregorio
Creek, you will have a half mile uphill, the first of three such climbs on
this part of the route. Although traffic is frequently heavy, the shoulder
is adequate, and you will have the ocean on one side and open countryside on the other to help compensate for the noise of automobiles.

In about 1.5 miles is Pomponio State Beach, named for an Indian
bandit who terrorized the coastside after escaping from the local
mission. Another 3 miles of riding will bring you to Pescadero State
Beach and Pescadero Marsh Natural Preserve. There is also a small
beach a little further on, directly opposite the road inland to the town
of Pescadero. If you have resisted the other beaches, you may want to
stop here to watch the waves roll in against the rocks or to look for sea
lions offshore.

It is possible to cut the mileage of the ride in half by going directly to the town of Pescadero at this point, located about 2.5 miles inland. The main route, however, continues along Highway 1 toward Pigeon Point Lighthouse.

From here on, the terrain levels out. In just over a mile is Pebble Beach, once famous for agates, carnelians, jaspar, and other sea-polished stones. After this beach was discovered in the 1860's, wagon-loads of tourists came in search of the beautiful pebbles. Eventually, however, the owner of the property, Loren Coburn, attemped to block access to the beach by erecting a fence and no trespassing signs. The public tore them down, and the "Pebble Beach War" dragged on in the courts for years.

In 1894, Coburn built a 200-room, $150,000 luxury resort hotel overlooking the beach, but it remained vacant as court battles continued. Finally, in 1904 the hotel began operation, but few guests were willing to make the long and uncomfortable trip by carriage to this site. Within a few years the hotel closed permanently and was torn down. And so, while you contemplate this stretch of peaceful, open beach, imagine instead a large, three-story, red-roofed hotel here, and be grateful the state has taken control of the coastline.

In another mile is Bean Hollow Beach, which has restrooms but no drinking water. The ride continues on past fields of artichokes and brussel sprouts, old farm buildings, a nursery, and an occasional more modern beach home. In 3.5 miles you will come to **Pigeon Point Lighthouse**, although its tower is visible in the distance long before that. There are two entrances to Pigeon Point Road; the first takes you off Highway 1 and closer to the beach for a half mile before coming to the lighthouse. The second entrance is marked by a sign directing you to the hostel.

Standing 115 feet tall, Pigeon Point Lighthouse has been guiding mariners since 1871. It was built in response to several shipwrecks off the coast, including one which gave the point its name. In 1853, the clipper ship Carrier Pigeon ran aground near what was then called Whale Point for the Portuguese whaling community located there. Not long thereafter, this point of land was renamed in memory of the ill-fated vessel.

The lighthouse is built of unreinforced brick brought around the Horn and is the second tallest on the West Coast. The original first-order Fresnel lens is still in place in the tower, although it was disconnected in 1972. The Fresnel lens, named after its French inventor, consists of 1,008 glass prisms which concentrate the light source, thus allowing a low-intensity light to project a strong beam over a great distance. Fresnel devised seven orders, or sizes, of lenses, the first-order being the largest and most powerful. The light currently in use is similar to an airport beacon.

Each lighthouse has its own distinctive light pattern which makes it identifiable to passing ships. Pigeon Point's is a 10 second flash pattern (1.2 seconds of light and 8.8 seconds of darkness).

Today Pigeon Point is operated by the American Youth Hostels and is a wonderful overnight stop for bicyclists. The individual bungalows were first built as Coast Guard family residences but now provide inexpensive lodging for travelers of every age from all over the world. The 1902 fog signal building has been converted to a recreation room for guests.

Call the hostel (415-879-0633) for information and reservations. The hostel is closed each day from 9:30 am to 4:30 pm, but the grounds are open to visitors. Tours of the lighthouse are given every Sunday for a small fee. Call the hostel for reservations.

Leave the lighthouse by returning the way you came, going north along Highway 1. You will most likely encounter headwinds going this direction, but soon you will escape both the wind and the traffic. In 2 miles, angle right, off the highway and onto Bean Hollow Road. (A blue sign reading "disposal site" also marks the turn.) This quiet road climbs one mile past open fields. Be careful on the downhill—the road is narrow and the surface rough. At the intersection with Pescadero Road, turn right for the short ride inland to the town of **Pescadero**.

For centuries the Ohlone Indians lived in this area, finding abundant food in the creeks and ocean, but the Indian population virtually disappeared during the Spanish mission period. In 1833 the land became part of Rancho El Pescadero ("the fishing place") when it was granted to Juan Jose Gonzales, majordomo at the Santa Cruz Mission.

The town itself was established in 1856 and first inhabited by farmers, ranchers and lumbermen. By the 1860's, Pescadero had a population of several hundred people and resembled a neat New England village. Many of the early residents came from Maine and constructed homes in the style of architecture of that area.

Pescadero's period of greatest activity occurred in the latter part of the 19th century when it was a popular resort community. Visitors came for the excellent hunting and fishing or in search of the pretty stones at nearby Pebble Beach. Millionaires such as the Floods and Crockers often drove their carriages over the mountains to enjoy these unspoiled surroundings. By the late 1800's there were two good hotels in town, the Swanton House and the Pescadero Hotel, and they were booked months in advance.

But Pescadero's prominence soon faded. The advent of the automobile in the early 1900's gave travelers greater access to places farther away. Fires destroyed much of the business district in the 1920's, and with the building of the coast highway, traffic bypassed the town. Pescadero reverted to the quiet little village you see today.

The intersection of Pescadero Road and Stage Road, where the flagpole is located, was once the heart of the business district. Go right to start your tour of some of the town's historic structures.

First, on the left, is the former Methodist-Episcopal Church. It was built in 1890 after the original structure north of Pescadero Road burned down. By 1905 the local Methodist membership could no longer support a pastor and sold the building. It was used as a community social center and then a Japanese cultural center until December 1941, when it became a movie theater. Today, it is owned by the Native Sons and Daughters of the Golden West.

Next door, at #110, is the former I.O.O.F. Hall. The International Order of Odd Fellows constructed the back part in 1878, while a front section, including veranda and porch, was added later. It is now a private residence.

The 1890's house at #94 shows several Victorian details. Of special interest is the lacy woodwork along the gable ridge. The house at #80 was built by Thomas Moore, the younger brother of the town's first

Thomas Moore House

settler, Alexander Moore. It probably dates from 1863 when Thomas was married. Notice the pierced columns of the porch and single-story kitchen wing at the back.

At the end of the block are the buildings of the I.D.E.S. (Irmandade do Dovino Espirito Santo), the Brotherhood of the Divine Holy Spirit. This Portuguese religious society sponsors the Festival of the Holy Ghost each spring, in which a parade and barbecue are the main events.

Bicycle back toward the flag pole, cross Pescadero Road, and ahead you will see the most famous establishment in town. Duarte's Tavern was started in 1895 when Frank Duarte had a barrel of whiskey brought from Santa Cruz. Since then, business has thrived through four generations of the Duarte family. The restaurant, especially noted for its artichoke soup and olallieberry pie, is open daily from 7:30 am to 9:00 pm and is a favorite stop for bicyclists.

Across the street from Duarte's is the site of the Swanton Hotel, which burned to the ground in the late 1920's. All that remains of this once popular resort is the magnificent magnolia tree behind the service station. There are several other businesses located on Stage Road, but perhaps the most important for cyclists is Arcangeli Grocery, opened in 1929. Fresh baked bread, as well as other food and picnic supplies, can be found here.

At the end of the block is the 1867 Pescadero Community Church, the oldest surviving Protestant church on the Peninsula still on its original site. When built, it had just a square bell tower above the entry, but in 1890 the steeple was added, making it the tallest building in Pescadero. Although constructed of redwood, the siding is scored to simulate stone. The church is open for services each Sunday at 11:00 am.

Across the street from the church, nearly hidden by trees, is the house James McCormick built in the late 1860's. McCormick was from Ireland and owned several businesses in Pescadero, including a hotel.

Turn right at the corner onto North Street, toward the residential part of town. Go right again at Goulson, originally the Spanish trail to the crossing over Pescadero Creek. The attractive home at #172 was built by Bartlett Weeks in 1885 and is still occupied by the third generation of the Weeks family. The log cabin across the street, however, is a Boy Scout project of more recent vintage.

Return to North Street, going right, and continue past Saint Anthony's Catholic Church, which dates from 1906. Down the street on the right is the old Pescadero high school, used from 1925 until 1960, when it was replaced with a new building located on Cloverdale Road.

When North Street intersects with Pescadero Road, you may wish to go left a short distance to Phipps Ranch. Here you can find all sorts of produce, dried beans, and herbs. Picnickers are welcome, and there are many farm animals to see. Phipps Ranch is open every day.

This was also the site of the 1855 Alexander Moore house, the first American home built in Pescadero. The 14-room house was constructed of lumber hauled from Santa Cruz. Unfortunately, it was destroyed by fire in 1975.

On the one mile ride back into town, Cloverdale Road intersects from the left. If you plan to camp in the area, Butano State Park is located 4.5 miles away on this road. The park rangers will always find space for those who arrive by bicycle.

Near town, on the right, is an old one-room schoolhouse at #2307 Pescadero Road. In 1875, because of dissatisfaction with the public school, John Garretson built his own private schoolhouse to educate his children. It was used only briefly for that purpose, however, and in 1885 was moved from the south end of Stage Road to this site. Today it provides housing for local workers. This building and Seaside School in San Gregorio are the two earliest surviving elementary schools on the Peninsula.

Next door is the Braddock Weeks house, dating from the 1860's. Weeks was one of the many Pescadero farmers who grew potatoes for the San Francisco market. As you near the flag pole and intersection with Stage Road, you will pass the Pescadero Store on the right. This is a modern restoration of what was once an early hotel and saloon.

Turn right on Stage Road and, once again, ride down the main street. As you leave Pescadero, make one last stop at Mt. Hope Cemetery, located on the hill past North Street. The cemetery was founded in 1875 by the I.O.O.F. Today half of it is owned by the Community Church and half by St. Anthony's Catholic Church. Many of Pescadero's pioneer settlers are buried here. Although it seems dry and barren much of the year, the cemetery is beautiful when the pink lilies called "naked ladies" bloom in August.

Before Highway 1 was constructed closer to the coast, Stage Road was the main connection between Pescadero and San Gregorio. The 7-mile ride along Stage Road is hilly but also provides some wonderful views, unless fog obscures the coast. You will have two significant climbs of one mile each, but that means you also have two good downhills. As you near the bottom of the second, you will see what is left of the town of San Gregorio. Don't miss the one-room Seaside School on the knoll to your right. It dates from the 1870's.

San Gregorio was once a well-known resort community, but now has shrunk to a population of less than 200. Remaining from this earlier time is the San Gregorio House, an old hotel with full-length balcony, located between San Gregorio Creek and Highway 84. It was built in 1866 by George Washington Carter on what was then the stage road to Pescadero. It was enlarged in 1875 by a new owner and for many years was filled with tourists who came for hunting, fishing or just relaxing. The hotel was finally closed in the 1930's, after the town was bypassed by the new coast highway. Today it is a private residence. On the corner in front of the hotel is a dilapidated service station, but before Prohibition, this was a saloon. It now stands empty.

San Gregorio Store

Across Highway 84 is the the Peterson & Alsford General Store, most commonly called the **San Gregorio Store**, the main attraction in town. You can find almost anything you want here—food, beverages, clothes, books, kitchen equipment, hardware, and more. (There is also a restroom.) Bicyclists are welcome, but please use the bike rack; don't lean your bicycle against the building.

After browsing through the general store, it is time to return to your starting point, less than a mile away. Ride on Highway 84 toward the ocean, and when you reach Highway 1, go left to the San Gregorio State Beach parking lot. This completes your exploration of the San Mateo County coast and its historic country villages.

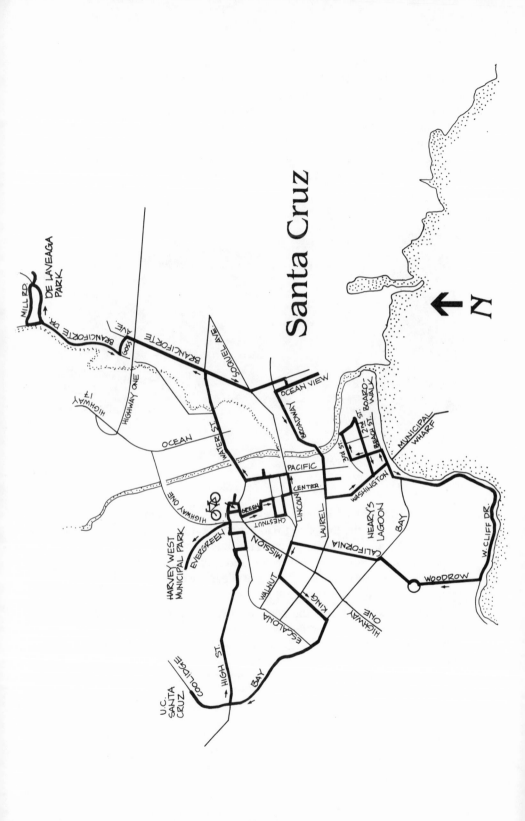

Santa Cruz

Distance: 18.5 miles

Rating: This **moderately strenuous** route is mostly along bike lanes or bike paths, but has numerous short hills, some of which are quite steep. Traffic, both automobile and pedestrian, may be heavy near the Boardwalk and downtown. It is strongly recommended that you do not do this ride during the summer, especially on weekends, when the city is crowded with visitors and leisurely cycling almost impossible.

Highlights: On this varied ride you can explore the history of Santa Cruz from its mission and pueblo beginnings to its heyday as a popular turn-of-the-century resort community. Included are splendid Victorians, old adobes, the renewed downtown mall, a pioneer cemetery, vestiges of the 19th century Cowell Ranch (now part of UC Santa Cruz), and a pleasant ride along the ocean.

Begin your ride where Santa Cruz began, at the mission. From Highway 17, take Highway 1 toward Half Moon Bay. You can see the white steepled church on Mission Hill from the highway. Turn left on Mission Street (after the pedestrian overpass) and left again on Emmet Street, on the far side of Plaza Park, the center of the mission quadrangle. Park your car along here.

Mission La Exaltacion de la Santa Cruz was first established on the flatland along the San Lorenzo River in 1791 but, being endangered by frequent floods, was moved to its hilltop location two years later. The city of Santa Cruz owes its origins not only to the mission, however, but also to the Villa de Branciforte. Founded in 1797 on the bluff across the river from the mission, this settlement was the last and least prosperous of the three civil pueblos established by the Spanish in early California.

From the start, the pueblo gave the mission padres trouble. Many of the original colonists were paroled criminals and disabled pensioned soldiers who indulged in drinking, gambling and other worldly behavior. These secular pleasures soon became more popular with the Indian neophytes than church work, and the mission was faced with desertion by much of its labor force.

In 1818, afraid that Santa Cruz would be attacked by the pirate De Bouchard, who had previously sacked Monterey, the padres fled to the safety of the Santa Clara Mission. They left the colonists of the Pueblo Villa de Branciforte to guard the mission at Santa Cruz. Although a storm at sea kept the pirate from landing, the padres returned to find the mission damaged and its supplies stolen by the guards.

Heavy rains and secularization brought further decay, and the mission church finally collapsed in 1857 after a series of earthquakes. The present Mission Santa Cruz, a half-size replica of the original, was constructed in 1931.

The only remaining building from the original mission complex is an adobe located one block down School Street, off Emmet. This adobe was part of a row of one-room apartments that housed Indian converts and dates from the 1820's. It is currently in the process of restoration by the state and is scheduled for completion in time for Santa Cruz's bicentennial in 1991. From the end of School Street there is a good view overlooking the town.

Return to Emmet, and continue around the Plaza on High Street to Holy Name Catholic Church, the building visible from the highway. It is located on the site of the original mission chapel. This Gothic style church was completed in 1889. The granite triple arch in front was erected in 1891 to commemorate the 100 year anniversary of the founding of Mission Santa Cruz.

From the church, turn left onto Sylvar Street. The small saltbox house at #109 was built about 1850 and is the oldest wood frame house in Santa Cruz. Francisco Alzina, first sheriff of Santa Cruz County, and his wife Maria, raised 14 children here. Dwarfing the Alzina house is the spacious Willey home next door, at #105, dating from 1887. Across the street, at #207 Mission, is probably the finest example of Eastlake style Victorian architecture still standing in Santa Cruz. Built in 1883, it presents an imposing facade with its three-and-a-half story tower.

Go right on Mission noting the twin 1867 cottages at #214 and #218. Louis Schwartz built these homes as rental units. His own larger residence, with even more gingerbread trim, is next door at #222. It dates from 1865.

Turn left immediately onto Green Street. Two houses of interest here are #127, a charming little clapboard home from the late 1860's, and #123 next door. Part of the latter residence was built in 1850 as the Methodist Church, the first Protestant church in Santa Cruz. Originally located at the corner of Mission and Green, it was moved to this site in 1864, after being replaced by a larger building. The house has been altered and enlarged over the years, but is still very attractive, particularly in its current setting.

At the bottom of Green Street, cross the road, angling left onto Union Street. The train tracks here are used by Roaring Camp and Big

Trees Railway, who operate a train along the century-old route from Felton to the Santa Cruz Boardwalk during the months of May to October. Call 408-335-4484 for information.

In one block, turn right onto Center Street and right again in 2 blocks onto Church Street. This will take you past the Santa Cruz City Hall built in the 1930's around a landscaped Spanish courtyard with tiled fountains and gardens in bloom year round. The building occupies the site of the 1872 Frederick A. Hihn mansion, which was probably the largest, most expensive and most elaborate house ever constructed in the city. The house was used as the city hall from 1920 until it was demolished after completion of the present building.

Frederick Hihn came to California from Germany in 1848 to mine gold. He settled in Santa Cruz in 1851, eventually investing in real estate and becoming chief developer and foremost financier of the town. He is credited with creating a county water system and building county streets and railroads. His first home, erected in 1857, is still standing at #324 Locust Street, but is now greatly altered. Several other houses in the neighborhood were built for members of his family.

At the end of Church Street is #529 Chestnut, an impressive Eastlake Victorian from 1888. Turn left and then left again onto Walnut Avenue. This street is lined with charming and beautifully restored 19th century homes, part of the most fashionable neighborhood of its time.

Calvary Episcopal Church

127

Go right, back onto Center, and then left on Lincoln Street. On the corner here is the 1864 Gothic style Calvary Episcopal Church, the oldest known church building in continuous use in California. The stained glass windows are of special note. The belfry was added in 1874, and the additional church buildings are 20th century.

Down the block on the left, at #208 Lincoln, is the childhood home of actress Zasu Pitts. She started her career in high school plays held at the old Opera House. Her home dates from the 1870's.

At the end of the next block, turn left onto **Pacific Garden Mall**, the center of downtown Santa Cruz. Prior to 1969, this street was a deteriorating business district. Now, thanks in large part to the efforts of the late photographer Chuck Abbott, it is an attractive avenue, with slow moving traffic, a wide variety of trees and plants, and broad sidewalks that encourage browsing the shops and restaurants lining the street. If traffic seems heavy here or you wish to spend some time sightseeing, you may want to walk your bicycle along the sidewalk.

The architectural highlight of the mall is the Cooper House located at the corner of Pacific Avenue and Cooper Street. The imposing style of this structure is known as Richardsonian Romanesque Revival. Built as the County Court House in 1894, it now houses a collection of shops and restaurants, with live music frequently featured in the front courtyard.

A short block down Cooper Street is the uniquely shaped brick **Octagon Museum.** This was the County Hall of Records from 1882 to 1968 before becoming the county historical museum. Its shape is said to have been modeled after that of a U.S. gold piece from the 1850's. The small museum is open Tuesday through Sunday, from noon to 5:00 pm.

Return to Pacific Avenue. There are a number of old commercial buildings along this street dating from the 1870's to the early 1900's, variously constructed of wood, brick and cast iron. Take your time exploring Pacific Garden Mall, as the variety of people taking their leisure here is at least as interesting as the historic buildings.

As you reach the end of the mall, walk your bicycle along the sidewalk on the lefthand side of the street until you reach the traffic light. Across the intersection you will see the City Clock, which once stood on top of the I.O.O.F. building. It was placed here in 1976 as part of the town's Bicentennial celebration. It makes a striking landmark.

Go to the right here onto Mission/Water Street. This is a busy thoroughfare, but has a bike lane. You will first cross the San Lorenzo River, named by Portola in 1769, and then Branciforte Creek. In less than a mile, at the top of a block-long hill, turn left onto Branciforte Avenue, following the sign to De Laveaga Park. This intersection was the center of Villa de Branciforte, and the mile-long straight Branciforte Avenue was laid out in 1797 as a racetrack.

The only remaining building of the pueblo is located just over half a mile along Branciforte at #1351, on the corner of Goss Avenue, after you cross over Highway 1. Situated behind the wall is the old two-room adobe building. Although enlarged over the years and partially covered with redwood siding, it still offers a reminder of what life was like in the pueblo days.

Go left on Goss, turning right in one block onto Market Street, which becomes Branciforte Drive. As you ride up the hill and along the tree-lined road following the creek, you begin to escape the city traffic.

In less than a mile you will reach the entrance to De Laveaga Park. Formerly the country estate of San Francisco millionaire J. V. De Laveaga, the land here was left to the city in 1894. Besides picnic facilities and restrooms, the park has an interesting old covered bridge. The 88-foot wooden structure was built in 1892 and moved to the park from its original location over Branciforte Creek a short distance away.

When you've had a chance to relax and perhaps enjoy a picnic lunch, leave the park, turning right. Immediately go left onto Mill Road, named for a brick mill once located here. This quiet country road recalls Santa Cruz's rural past. In contrast to the ramshackle farm buildings along the way is the former Rapetta ranch house at #99. Built in 1890 in the Queen Anne style, it now serves as a retirement home.

At the end of Mill Road, turn left onto Glen Canyon Road, then right, back onto Branciforte Drive. Return to busy Santa Cruz the way you came, going left on Goss and right on Branciforte Avenue. Cross the main streets of Water, Soquel and Broadway. One block past Broadway, a right turn onto Windsor Street will bring you to **Ocean View Avenue**, the prime residential street on the East Side since it was developed in 1871.

The views of Monterey Bay and the beach have been almost entirely blocked by construction at the end of the street, but the homes themselves have lost none of their elegance. Turn left on Ocean View and ride down the block and back, admiring the many large, well maintained dwellings.

Perhaps the most impressive of these is #250 Ocean View, on the corner of Windham Street. Built in 1891 for a Captain Gray, it was acquired in 1894 by Judge Lucas Smith. Lovingly restored by later owners, it still has its original wooden fence and carriage house. Of special note also is #245, a mixed Eastlake-Italianate style building from 1877.

Pedal up Ocean View to Broadway, turning left. In a block you will pass the Santa Cruz Hostel, at #511, housed in a five-bedroom Victorian. Call 408-423-8304 after 5:00 pm if you want to spend the night. Broadway, in contrast with sedate Ocean View, is a busy street with little room for bicyclists. In a few blocks, however, as you cross back over the San Lorenzo River, Broadway becomes Laurel, and you have a bike lane once again.

Smith House

After the street narrows to two lanes, turn left onto Cedar Street. At the end of the block, at #101, is the Blackburn House, a Greek Revival house from 1854. It is now a motel with three rooms in the main house and several more in surrounding cottages.

William Blackburn, for whom the house was built, was a participant in the Bear Flag Revolt in Sonoma. During his lifetime he was a gold miner, hotel and store keeper, potato grower, orchardist, mayor, justice of the peace, and, finally, judge. By the time he died in 1867, he had extensive landholdings and was recognized as the wealthiest citizen of Santa Cruz.

Return on Cedar to Laurel, turning left. At the next corner, at #319, note the 1887 Four Palms apartment building, with its elaborate sawn-wood ornamentation. In another block, turn left onto Washington Street. As you bicycle by the former Southern Pacific railroad depot, look up to your left for a glimpse of the old Hotel McCray, alone on Beach Hill. This was once a splendid home called Sunshine Villa, owned by millionaire James Smith and his wife (known for her role in organizing the Venetian Water Carnival of 1895 held on the San Lorenzo River). It later became a resort hotel but now stands abandoned and forlorn.

Washington Street ends at the Municipal Wharf. As you turn left onto Beach Street, you will see Santa Cruz's mile-long stretch of warm, sunny beach spread out before you. Down Beach Street is the famed Santa Cruz Boardwalk, a popular attraction since the turn of the century. The dance casino is at one end, and the 1924 roller coaster, the oldest full-sized attraction of this kind on the West Coast, at the other. The merry-go-round with its hand carved horses dates from 1910.

The early economy of Santa Cruz was based on lumbering, limestone quarrying, cattle raising, agriculture, and fishing. But these gave way to the importance of the resort trade by the mid-1860's. The mild climate, sunny summer weather, and beautiful beaches attracted large numbers of vacationers. Although the resort era peaked early in this century, the beaches and Boardwalk still draw crowds of tourists today.

Since bicycles are not allowed on the Boardwalk, take the first left off Beach, but gear down, for Main Street starts with a short, but very steep, incline. This route will take you into the heart of Beach Hill, the resort center of Santa Cruz for over a century.

In the next block, just past a large Victorian home, are the Carmelita Cottages. This collection of 1870's vacation cottages is tucked away off the street, at #321. Now a city park, plans are underway to convert these buildings to a hostel by summer of 1990. For information, call 408-423-8304.

At the end of the block, at #924 Third Street, is the massive Golden Gate Villa. A number of changes have been made to the house over the years, the most apparent being enclosure of the tower. When built in 1891 for Major Frank McLaughlin, the third story of the tower was entirely open, with columns and arches. In contrast to its relatively simple exterior, the interior of this house was the most lavish of any in Santa Cruz. A tragic story is associated with this impressive residence, however. In 1907, two years after his wife's death, McLaughlin shot his stepdaughter Agnes and ended his own life with cyanide. The motive for his actions remains a mystery.

Turn right onto Third and ride 2 blocks to the corner of Cliff Street. At #417 Cliff is another spectacular building of the period. It was constructed in 1899 for banker H. S. Deming and his family. Like Golden Gate Villa and other large homes in the area, it has been converted into apartments. In another block, at #611 Third, is Rio Vista, a Stick-Eastlake style residence constructed in 1890 and known for its ten stained glass windows.

Go right on Liebrandt Avenue, following the road right as it turns onto Second Street. Continue uphill on Second, turning left when it ends at Washington. When you reach the corner, go right onto Beach

Street, and head up the hill. At the top, angle left at this congested intersection onto West Cliff Drive.

Located here, at #170 West Cliff Drive, is the Lynch House, the finest example of the Italianate style in Santa Cruz. It was the second largest home in the city when built in 1877 for Sedgewich Lynch, a general contractor who had struck it rich in the gold fields. Today, the once magnificent residence is surrounded by modern commercial establishments, and seems sadly out of place.

When you reach the stop sign at the end of the block, cross to the left to get on the two-way bike path along West Cliff Drive. Here you will have a pleasant and relaxing 1.5 mile ride along the ocean, unless it is a busy summer day, in which case you will be competing with all manner of roller skaters, joggers and skateboarders. Regardless, you will have fine views of the Municipal Wharf, beach, and Boardwalk.

Several large turn-of-the-century homes are located along this street. At #314 is a Mission Revival style residence built about 1910 by Watsonville architect William Weeks. It is now a bed and breakfast inn. The 1897 house next door, at the corner of Santa Cruz Avenue and West Cliff, had been purchased a number of years earlier by Bishop and Mrs. Warren of Colorado for use as a summer home. The newer dwelling was built for their son.

Further along, at #544, is a building that serves as the Oblates of St. Joseph residence house. It was once the colonial style mansion, Rutherglen Terrace, built in 1893 for James McNeil, owner and president of the Santa Cruz Electric Light and Power Works.

The small lighthouse on Santa Cruz Point is definitely worth a stop. The first lighthouse was built here in 1869. The present building was erected by Chuck and Esther Abbott in memory of their son Mark, who died in a body surfing accident in 1965. The lighthouse contains the Santa Cruz **Surfing Museum,** open from 10:00 am to 5:00 pm, Tuesday through Saturday, and noon to 5:00 pm Sunday. Seal Rock, off the point, is home to a colony of sea lions.

Continue on the bike path until you come to Woodrow Avenue. (A stop sign marks its intersection with West Cliff Drive.) Although the bike path continues all the way to Natural Bridges State Park, a right turn at this corner will take you toward the area known as The Circles. This neighborhood dates from 1890 when the Christian Church built a tabernacle, and roads were laid out in concentric circles around it. Developed haphazardly, the area is now mostly a curiosity.

As you reach the present Christian Church, which replaced the original tabernacle, go right on Errett Circle, and take the next right onto California Avenue. When the street ends, go left on Bay Street, then immediately right onto California again. This will take you by Nearys Lagoon Park and Wildlife Refuge. (Restrooms are available here.)

Ride along California a few blocks to #724, one of Santa Cruz's truly spectacular Victorians. Built in 1886 for Thomas Jefferson Weeks, the entire surface seems covered with moldings, brackets, and sawn-wood trim of flutings, scrolls and swirls. The house originally stood on Walnut Avenue but was moved to this location in 1913 to make way for Santa Cruz High School.

Continue to the end of the street, turning left on Walnut and taking note of the interesting old homes here. Cross Mission Street, and in 2 blocks, go left on King Street. Don't miss #1104 on the corner of Laurent Street. With its polygonal tower, it is a neighborhood landmark. Turn right on Bay Street, which soon becomes divided Bay Drive. A mile long uphill ride will bring you to the campus of the **University of California at Santa Cruz**, site of the old Cowell Ranch.

At the top of the rise, you will see open meadows and old ranch buildings ahead. As you cross High Street and enter the campus, Bay becomes Glenn Coolidge Drive. On the left is the old horse barn, now converted to a campus theater. Take the first right into the short driveway leading to the former granary, today a child care center, and to the stonehouse, once the ranch paymaster's house. From here you will also have the best view of the simple Cowell ranch house up on the hill.

Henry Cowell came to California during the gold rush and acquired miles of property up and down the coast, including this ranch where he quarried lime and raised cattle. He lived here with his wife and five children from 1865 to 1897. Cowell was extremely wealthy and ruled his family with an iron hand, decreeing that none of his children should marry. When one son did so, he was ostracized by the family until the marriage ended.

Before Samuel Henry Cowell, the last surviving child, died in 1955, he established a foundation to distribute the family's wealth. The Cowell Foundation helped fund health centers at several universities, donated land near Felton for Henry Cowell Redwoods State Park, and made 2000 acres of the ranch property available for this university campus, which opened in the early 1960's.

Return to Coolidge Drive and ride up the hill past more old ranch buildings. The redwood and stone cookhouse on the left is now the campus admissions office. The dilapidated cabins on the ridges once housed ranch workers. The long frame building on stone piers was the cooperage, and beyond are wood-burning stone lime kilns, which may have been constructed as early as 1851. A blacksmith shop is located up the road.

Cowell Ranch Cooperage and Lime Kilns

Opposite the driveway on the right, which leads to the Cowell carriage house, is the entrance to a bicycle path. If you wish, you may ride the one mile path to the various university buildings attractively situated amongst redwood trees. Two more historic buildings, the powder house and slaughterhouse, are located along the route.

When you are ready to leave, take Coolidge Drive down to its intersection with High Street, turning left at the stop sign. Follow High downhill, going right on Storey Street near the bottom. In one block make a left turn onto Escalona Drive and then left again on Highland Avenue. Take note of #203, on the corner, an unusual 1882 house with a three-story tower.

A right at the next corner will put you back onto High Street. Piedmont Court is located here, an impressive two-story Mission Revival-Moorish design apartment building constructed around an interior court complete with fountain. It was built in 1912.

At the end of High Street, take a left onto the bike path along the fence, which will bring you to Evergreen Street. Go straight ahead here, following the road a short distance to the fascinating cool and overgrown Evergreen Cemetery, established in 1858.

Built on the sides of a steep hill, the cemetery is divided into five sections, including one for Civil War veterans, members of the Grand Army of the Republic. The most interesting part, however, is that for Chinese, highest up the hill and most inaccessible. The large brick oven used for burning clothes of the deceased during the funeral service still remains, as does the wooden platform where the ceremonies took place. If you like exploring pioneer cemeteries, this one will keep you busy a long time.

At the end of Evergreen Street is Harvey West Municipal Park with picnic and restroom facilities. It also has some displays of early California history, such as an overland stage which carried U.S. mail.

Return the way you came, up the short but steep bike path. When you reach High Street, walk your bicycle up the pedestrian overpass which crosses Highway 1. On the other side is Mission Plaza, where your exploration of historic Santa Cruz first began.

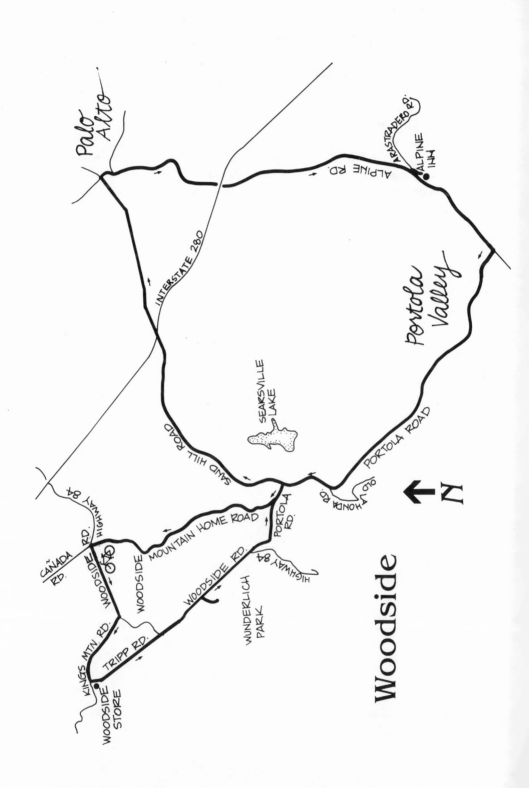

Woodside

Distance: 6.5 miles with 12 mile optional addition

Rating: The short route is mostly **easy**, taking place on narrow roads that are flat to gently rolling. Traffic may be heavy on Woodside Road, however, so you will need some bicycling experience to enjoy this ride. The additional loop is rated **moderate**. It adds only one real climb and one very busy intersection. Otherwise, you will ride on pleasant country roads, many of which are tree-lined and shady.

Highlights: One of the most popular routes for area bicyclists, this ride will take you through scenic wooded and open countryside. You will trace the history of Woodside, site of the first English-speaking settlement on the Peninsula, from its origins as a lumbering town to its more recent emergence as a community of country estates. The longer route also takes you through Portola Valley, home of an historic tavern, as well as old estates of its own.

The early history of Woodside contrasts sharply to the affluent image it presents today. The first settlers, who began arriving in the early 1830's, were deserters who had jumped ship in San Francisco and Monterey. They were a rough but easygoing lot, boisterous, fond of drinking, and not much given to hard work. Some of these fugitives and drifters, however, began lumbering the redwoods, using sawpits, a crude forerunner of sawmills.

In 1840 John Copinger was awarded 12,000 acres of prime redwood land for his support of a successful coup by Governor Juan Alvarado. He was also appointed justice of the peace. Copinger's land grant, Rancho Cañada de Raymundo, became a center of activity during the 1840's. The demand for lumber and shingles was great, providing plenty of work for the local sawyers. A number of corn liquor stills also began appearing in the woods and did a lively business, apparently encouraged by Copinger.

Despite occasional attempts by the Mexican and United States governments to evict and deport the "undesirables," the vagabond community continued to survive until the outbreak of the Mexican War in 1846. At that time U.S. Marines invaded Cañada de Raymundo, conscripting men and seizing horses and cattle. Copinger died shortly after the annexation of California by the U.S. When lumbering was resumed after the Gold Rush, and the West Coast's first sawmills were introduced, the old crowd was gone and an era had ended.

In 1850 Copinger's widow, Maria Luisa Soto, married a very different sort of man. John Greer was a stern Irish Presbyterian sea captain whose crew had abandoned ship for the gold fields in 1849. To combat the continuing whiskey problem (for which his predecessor no doubt was partly responsible), he helped form a local temperance society and also donated land for a school. Woodside's rough and tumble ways were beginning to change.

Begin your ride in the center of Woodside, at the intersection of Woodside Road (Highway 84) and Cañada Road. There is parking at the back of the lot behind the shopping center. You will probably see many other cyclists here, buying food at Roberts Store, filling water bottles outside, or just passing through on their way to the coast or on the route you will be following. You are also likely to encounter equestrians, as Woodside seems to have nearly as many horses as people.

The center of the Woodside settlement moved from the base of the Santa Cruz Mountains to this location after lumbering declined in the mid-1860's. The demand created by the frantic building boom in San Francisco after the Gold Rush had quickly stripped the area of its virgin redwood, and cutting had been forced to move over the ridge. By the 1880's there were several stores and three saloons here, giving the area its name of Whiskey Hill. The old Pioneer Hotel, which can be found one block east at the intersection with Whiskey Hill Road, was built in 1882. Although only the facade is from the original building, it still houses a saloon, along with offices.

Leave the center of town heading west toward the mountains on shady Woodside Road. Just past the library on the right is the quaint Church of the Redeemer. Constructed as a Congregational church in 1891, it now serves as a chapel for the newer church next door. Across the street, adjacent to the school, is Independence Hall, dating from 1884. Originally located a few blocks away, it was used for public gatherings and later for scout meetings.

In just over half a mile, turn right on King's Mountain Road, at the signs for Huddart Park and Woodside Store. This intersection was called Adobe Corner when the original Copinger residence was located here. King's Mountain Road, built in 1869 as a lumberman's toll road, is narrow, but traffic is light and fairly slow moving. In another half a mile, just before crossing Union Creek, notice the Charles Josselyn House, at #400, on the right. It is situated behind a low stone wall and nearly hidden by trees. This attractive one-story villa, built in 1906, provides an example of the country estates that were constructed in this area in the early 1900's.

At the junction with Tripp Road is the historic **Woodside Store**, one of the few surviving landmarks from Woodside's pioneer days. Restored and rebuilt by the County of San Mateo, the museum is operated by the San Mateo County Historical Association and is open free of charge on Tuesday, Thursday, Saturday, and Sunday, from noon to 5:00 pm. Of special interest is an antique penny farthing bicycle on display.

The present structure was built on land owned by Mathias Parkhurst, who operated a redwood shingle mill with his partner Robert Orville Tripp, a dentist. As more and more mills were established, they decided to give up the lumber business and in 1851 opened a store in a crude lean-to. Three years later they constructed the redwood building you see today.

The store, the only one between San Francisco and Santa Clara, quickly became the center of activity for the lumbering community which later became known as Woodside. At one time there were 15 sawmills within a five mile radius of the store, and more than 1,000 lumberjacks bought their food, supplies and liquor here. The store also served as a post office, bank, library, and, of course, dentist's office.

Woodside Store

139

Tripp acquired the property after Parkhurst died in 1863 and continued to operate the store until his death in 1909 at age 93. The business remained prosperous, despite the decline in the logging business. As agriculture, including vineyards, gradually developed in the valley, Tripp expanded his interests, building a winery behind the store and marketing his own brand, "The San Mateo County Pioneer."

By 1890 there were nearly 800 acres devoted to grape growing in the Woodside area, and several small wineries had been established. Prohibition brought an end to that industry, however, and now the land has been put to other uses.

When you are ready to leave the Woodside Store, continue riding along quiet, shady Tripp Road. Here, again, you will catch glimpses of the estates, mansions and stables for which Woodside is now known. Its scenic charm and warm climate attracted many wealthy San Franciscans in the late 1800's and have been drawing the rich and famous ever since.

Unfortunately for sightseers, most of the old estates along here are set well back off the road and are hidden from view. There is a pair of interesting church-like red brick structures near the road, however, in about half a mile. Part of the Whittell estate, one was a theater for Mrs. Whittell, a French actress who apparently was not accepted by proper Woodside society. The other housed her collection of wild animals.

On the high rise of ground on the other side of the road was the location of the Temperance Hall built by Greer and Tripp. It was also the community social hall where weekly dances were held.

In another half mile, Tripp Road rejoins Woodside Road, and you go right. Traffic may be heavy here, as Highway 84 carries beach goers to the coast, but the shoulder is mostly adequate. In just over half a mile, near the end of a gradual downhill, turn right into the entrance of **Wunderlich County Park** to see the remnants of another fine estate.

This former ranch land was purchased in 1902 by James Folger II, the coffee tycoon, and used for weekend excursions and campouts. His mansion still stands but is not on park property. You can, however, see the handsome stable he built, still in use today. The park is named for Martin Wunderlich, who obtained much of the Folger estate in 1956 and donated the park land to San Mateo County in 1974.

Leaving the park, continue along Woodside Road for another half mile. Just as Highway 84 begins its climb up the Santa Cruz Mountains, go left onto Portola Road. Use caution as you turn, and watch for traffic coming down the hill.

The land to your left was once part of the 2000-acre Mountain Home Ranch, sold by Copinger to Charles Brown in 1846. Brown, a deserter from a whaling ship, had built an adobe on the property possibly as early as 1838. The small square adobe, thought to be the oldest building in San Mateo County, is still in good condition. Its red tile roof is just barely visible from the road. Brown is best remembered for installing the first sawmill on the Peninsula in 1847.

Ride along scenic Portola Road, lined with eucalyptus trees. The creek here is called Alambique, Spanish for "still," after one of the illegal distilleries in the mountains. The creek provided water power for Brown's mill until a steam boiler was installed. At the stop sign, go right, staying on Portola. Across the road at the next intersection and over the embankment is the site of the former town of Searsville, now covered by Searsville Lake.

The little town of **Searsville** grew up around an inn built by John Sears in 1854. The hotel served as a stopover for drivers of mule and ox teams hauling lumber from the mills to Redwood City. It was also the Sunday gathering place for the lumbermen who entertained themselves with such activities as horse racing, cockfighting, drinking, gambling and brawling.

By the 1870's the best timber had been cut, and Searsville was only a quiet farming village. Its end came in 1892 after the settlers lost a long legal battle with the Spring Valley Water Company, which planned to flood the area by damming San Francisquito Creek. After the work was completed, however, green algae were found in the water which made it undrinkable. Eventually, the lake was turned over to Stanford University as a source of irrigation water. It was also used for recreational purposes before becoming part of Stanford's Jasper Ridge Biological Preserve.

If you are doing the short ride, turn around here. When the road divides, stay to the right on Mountain Home Road. Follow this gently rolling, narrow country road for 2 miles back to the center of Woodside. Many of the fine estates along the way are not visible from the road except for their impressive entrance gates and paddocks, so you must use your imagination to picture them. As you ride along, you will probably find yourself reflecting on the changes Woodside has undergone since its humble beginnings.

Optional addition: From Searsville, turn east up Sand Hill Road. After a brief up and downhill, you will have a moderate climb of less than a mile. Traffic may be fast-moving here, but there is a wide, smooth shoulder. To the right you will have views of Jasper Ridge and the mile-long Stanford Linear Accelerator. The quick downhill is interrupted by the exit and entrance ramps over Interstate 280, so use caution. One last short climb brings you to the top of a rise, with views of Stanford

University's Hoover Tower, San Francisco Bay, and the East Bay hills beyond.

In one mile, just before the end of Sand Hill Road, look to your right to see the side entrance to the wooded grounds of the Meyer-Buck Estate, now willed to Stanford University. (You will be able to catch a glimpse of the house itself in a short distance.) On the opposite side of Sand Hill Road was the site of Sharon Heights, the extensive estate of Fred Sharon, a senator's son. All that remains today is an artificial lake of the Japanese gardens, now part of Sharon Park.

The intersection ahead with Santa Cruz Avenue and Alpine Road brings you to the busiest, most congested part of the ride. As you turn right on Alpine, you will suddenly find yourself with no shoulder, and you must merge with the traffic. But this condition lasts only for a short block, after which the traffic thins and the shoulder widens.

Just around the corner, pull off the road at the driveway and look up to see the large Mediterranean style house of the Meyer-Buck Estate. Built in the late 1800's for the J. Henry Meyer family, it was rebuilt in 1920 after a fire. One of the Meyer daughters, Alice Buck, lived here until her death in 1979.

Alpine Road is pleasant cycling but with a gentle incline. After going under Interstate 280 (again, watch for traffic at the exit/entrance ramps), you will pass the unincorporated community of Ladera and then enter the Portola Valley town limits.

Alpine Road was once an Indian trail linking the south bay clam-digging sites with the coast. During the 1840's, the trail was widened by Antonino Buelna to connect his San Gregorio ranch with his property on the future site of Stanford. As late as the 1870's, it remained the only direct route from the south bay to the coast.

Three miles from the turn onto Alpine Road is the historic **Alpine Inn**, California's oldest roadhouse in continuous operation. Using the left turn lane, go left onto Arastradero Road and immediately right into the driveway.

The history of this establishment dates back to 1852 when it was built by Buelna's son Felix. The tavern quickly became a hangout for the local inhabitants, who enjoyed gambling and bull-and-bear fights here.

In 1868 the building was sold to Irishman William Stanton to settle gambling debts, and was renamed Stanton's Saloon. After his death in 1887, his heirs leased the tavern to a Portuguese immigrant known as Black Chapete. He was a likeable man who enjoyed drinking with his customers, and his hospitality attracted a large clientele, especially after Stanford University opened in 1891. Despite attempts by Stanford officials to have the tavern closed to protect students from its influence, Black Chapete's thrived.

Alpine Inn

In the early 1900's the building was leased to a German who changed the name to *The Wunder*. The tavern survived Prohibition and acquired a new owner in the late 1940's, when it became Rossotti's. It has been the Alpine Inn since 1957, although still called "Zots" by many of its habitués.

The Alpine Inn, now a State Historical Landmark, remains a popular place, frequented by students, local residents and bicyclists, who enjoy sipping beer and eating hamburgers at the picnic tables in back. The Inn opens at 11:30 am every day.

From the Alpine Inn continue along Alpine Road for just over a mile, taking a right onto Portola Road where a sign directs you to Skyline Boulevard and Woodside. (Food is available at the shopping center just before the turn.) The next 3.5 miles are a gradual downhill through the comfortable suburb of **Portola Valley**.

This area was once remote enough to shelter Indians seeking to avoid mission life. As Rancho Corte Madera after 1833, it was used for cattle ranching. Farming and ranching continued to predominate until the mid-20th century. This included the raising of horses. The championship English race horse Ormonde was brought here in the late 19th century, and his progeny were trained at Ormondale Ranch.

But Portola Valley's most famous resident of the period was Andrew Hallidie, inventor of San Francisco's cable cars. He donated land for a school and post office, the beginning of the present settlement. He also used his ranch for further experiments, building an aerial cable tram-way from the valley floor into the mountains where his home was located.

There are several interesting landmarks to see along the road. In half a mile, a red windmill stands out on the right. Although the windmill itself was purely decorative, it housed the pump machinery for one of the oldest and deepest wells in the area.

A short distance further along, on the left, is an impressive castle-like gatehouse. This was built sometime after 1912 of wood faced with stones from Corte Madera Creek to house the superintendent of the Willow Brook estate, owned by Herbert Law. Law had made his fortune by formulating and selling a patent medicine for "ladies' problems," and bought the land to grow the special plants he needed for the elixir. His Roman style villa was razed in 1945, and only the gatehouse remains.

The valley widens here, giving you views of peaceful open fields and the Santa Cruz Mountains. Beneath you, however, is the San Andreas Fault, one of the most active earthquake faults in the country. Its presence is the reason much of this land has remained rural and undeveloped.

In just over half a mile on the left is the little red Portola Valley school-house, next to the Town Hall. It dates from 1912. Built of redwood in the Mission Revival style popular at the time, it is now an art gallery.

Portola Valley Schoolhouse

Next you will come to Our Lady of the Wayside Catholic Church, at #930 Portola Road, hidden behind a stand of redwoods on the right. Also built in 1912, this charming Mission-style edifice was designed by noted architect Timothy Pflueger.

Ride 2 more miles, passing the turnoff to Old La Honda Road. August Schilling, the spice merchant, once had his estate near this intersection. Follow Portola Road around a curve and past the Searsville Marsh, making a left turn just before the road begins to climb up Sand Hill. This is the way you came. When the road divides, stay to the right on Mountain Home Road.

Continue on Mountain Home 2 miles back to the center of Woodside, enjoying the last of your ride through this scenic rural community.

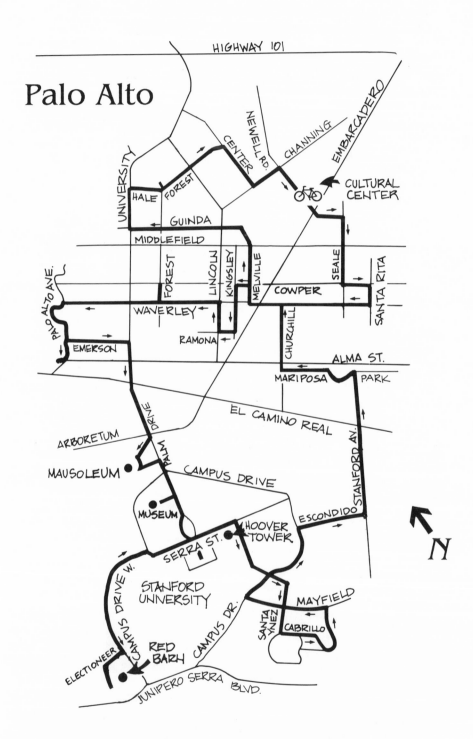

Palo Alto

Palo Alto

Distance: 14 miles with 2.5 mile optional side trip

Rating: The route is **easy**, taking place almost entirely on flat city streets, frequently with bike lanes. There is only one short incline in the Stanford faculty housing area. Traffic may be somewhat heavy near downtown and campus.

Highlights: On this ride you will explore the spacious campus of Stanford University. You will also see some attractive Palo Alto residential areas dating from the late 19th century, including historic Professorville, as well as gracious homes from later periods.

Begin your ride at the Palo Alto Cultural Center on Newell Road off Embarcadero Road, about one mile west of Highway 101. Originally built as the Palo Alto City Hall, it was used for that purpose until 1970, when the growth of the city required a move to larger quarters. As the Cultural Center, it is now an art gallery with changing exhibits, classes and other community events.

Start by riding left on Newell, crossing Embarcadero. In another block, turn right on Seale Avenue. Soon you will cross Middlefield Road, the main highway between San Jose and San Francisco prior to the 1850's.

When you reach Cowper Street in 4 blocks, go left. At #1990 is the 1932 home of Lucie Stern, one of Palo Alto's best-loved philanthropists. It was designed by noted local architect Birge Clark in the Spanish Colonial Revival style for which he is known. Complementing it is the house next door at #1950, designed by Clark for Mrs. Stern's daughter.

Make a right turn at the corner onto Santa Rita Avenue, then take another right on Waverley Street. In just over half a mile, as you cross Embarcadero Road again, you enter the area known as **Professorville**. Here in the midst of grain fields were built the first homes that made up the original town of Palo Alto. The houses were constructed in the early 1890's by the faculty of the newly opened Stanford University, who wished to own their own land rather than lease it from the school.

To see some of the finest of Professorville's homes, start by turning right onto Melville Street, just past Embarcadero. The stately 1894 residence at #433 was designed by Birge Clark's father, Arthur B. Clark, an art professor at Stanford University. Make a left at the corner of Cowper to contrast his work with his son's. The remarkable early California style building at #1247 Cowper was designed by Birge Clark in 1927 for authors Kathleen and Charles Norris. It is now the Stanford Newman Center.

Before going left in one block onto Kingsley Avenue, note the impressive home on the corner. #501 Kingsley was built in 1897 for Professor Fleugel, a Chaucerian scholar. In addition to an 8000-volume library, he had a brick vault to safeguard his research papers.

One of the best known homes in the district is at #450 Kingsley, a Queen Anne built in 1894 for Professor Sanford, one of the 15 original Stanford professors. He lived here until his death in 1948. The next block has several more large attractive Victorians.

Continue on Kingsley, taking a right on Ramona Street. Here you will find numerous excellent examples of the Craftsman brown shingle style of architecture from the early 1900's. The most historic is #1103 at the end of the block, which belonged to Alfred Seale, son of one of Palo Alto's early pioneers. It was built in 1903.

Sunbonnet House

Turn right onto Lincoln. At the next corner, stop at #1061 Bryant, to your left, to see what has long been called the Sunbonnet House for its gambrel-roofed entry. It was built in 1899 for Emma Kellogg and designed by distinguished Bay Area architect Bernard Maybeck.

Across the street, at #1044 Bryant, is the modest cottage that was the childhood home of Russell and Sigurd Varian, electronics inventors and founders of Varian Associates.

Palo Alto might be considered the birthplace of the Electronic Age, as it was here in 1911-1913 that Dr. Lee de Forest devised the first vacuum tube and oscillator. He worked from his laboratory on the corner of Emerson and Channing, not far away. The research was undertaken for Cyril Elwell, the wireless pioneer, who in 1908 built the first radio-telephone station on the west coast at his home on Cowper.

Continue riding down Lincoln for one more historic block. It, too, has several unique period homes to appreciate. Then leave Professorville by turning left onto Waverley Street.

In 3 blocks, on the corner of Homer Avenue and Waverley, is St. Thomas Aquinas Catholic Church. Built in the Gothic Revival style in 1901, it is the oldest standing church structure in Palo Alto. This beautiful building was featured in the opening scenes of the 1972 film classic, *Harold and Maude*.

A right turn at the next intersection onto Forest Avenue and one short block of riding brings you to #706 Cowper, the splendid **Downing House**. This is Palo Alto's finest example of Victorian architecture. It was built in 1894 for T. B. Downing, a member of both the school board and first city council. After many years of neglect, it has been restored and is now used for offices.

Return to Waverley, turning right. One block further along, to your left and facing Hamilton Avenue, is the Spanish Colonial Revival style Palo Alto Post Office. Designed by Birge Clark in 1932, it was one of the first Federal buildings in which this style of architecture was permitted. Plans were finally approved only because President and Mrs. Hoover, who were Stanford residents, intervened.

Cross University Avenue, the main artery of downtown Palo Alto, and ride on Waverley until it ends at Palo Alto Avenue. Turn to the left and follow Palo Alto Avenue along San Francisquito Creek, once the boundary between the pasture lands of San Francisco's Mission Dolores to the north and Mission Santa Clara to the south.

At the intersection with Alma Street, enter the tiny park on the right and ride along the gravel pathway. Next to the railroad bridge is **El Palo Alto**, the tall redwood tree which has given the town its name. It was here that Gaspar de Portola and his men camped in November 1769 after discovering San Francisco Bay. Originally a much larger double-trunked tree, it has long been a local landmark, first for the Costanoan Indians and then for Spanish explorers. Later, after mission lands were dispersed, it delineated the boundary between two ranchos.

To the east was Rancho Rinconada del Arroyo de San Francisquito, owned by Rafael Soto. This is where the town of Palo Alto was later laid out. To the west of the tree was Rancho San Francisquito, which was to become the location of Stanford University. That land was granted in 1839 to Antonino Buelna.

Return to Palo Alto Avenue, going left, and in one block take a right onto Emerson Street. At University Avenue, turn right. If traffic is heavy, you may wish to walk your bicycle along the sidewalk. At the next corner, take a moment to admire the decorative second-story facade of the old Fraternal Hall across the street at #140. It dates from 1898. Continue along University. When you reach the underpass, be sure to use the sidewalk bike lane, as the road here is extremely narrow and heavily traveled.

At #27 University, just on the other side of the underpass, is the 1918 Hostess House, now a popular restaurant. The building was designed by Julia Morgan, best known as the architect of the Hearst Castle in San Simeon. Originally located at Camp Fremont in Menlo Park, the Hostess House was moved to its present site in 1919 and used as the first municipally supported community center in the nation.

Continue riding on the sidewalk bike route over El Camino Real. University Avenue becomes Palm Drive as you enter the campus of **Stanford University**, built by Leland and Jane Stanford as a memorial to their only child, Leland Stanford Junior.

Leland Stanford came to California with his wife in 1852. He was elected governor in 1861, campaigning to keep California part of the Union at the time of the Civil War. As one of the "Big Four," he was responsible for the construction of the first transcontinental railroad, and in 1869 at Promontory Point, Utah, drove the golden spike that marked the joining of the Union Pacific railroad line from the east with the Central Pacific line from the west. He later served a term as United States Senator.

In 1876 the Stanfords purchased part of the old Buelna rancho for what would become the celebrated Palo Alto Stock Farm, the largest and most successful trotting horse establishment in the world. Here Governor Stanford bred and trained world championship trotters. He, along with the famous photographer Eadweard Muybridge, also conducted experiments that proved a trotter has all four feet off the ground at one instant in its stride.

Young Leland Junior also loved the farm, as well as his trips to Europe with his parents. But in 1884, while traveling in Italy, he died of typhoid fever. He was not yet 16 years old.

His grief-stricken parents decided to found a university in their son's memory on the grounds of the Palo Alto Farm. Leland Stanford Junior

University opened its doors in 1891 with 495 students. Today, it has over 12,000 students and is considered one of the finest institutions of higher education in the country.

Ride on the sidewalk bike path along Palm Drive for about 2 blocks. Just after crossing Arboretum Road, angle right onto the very rough pathway, which is nearly blocked by large logs. Soon you will see the statue known as Angel of Grief on your right. This is the grave site of Henry Lathrop, Mrs. Stanford's younger brother. Turn left to reach the Stanford family mausoleum. Here, guarded by four sphinxes, are the remains of Leland, Jane, and Leland Junior. The giant oak tree in front of the building was the favorite climbing tree of Leland Junior.

Leave this peaceful place by way of the wide path directly in front of the mausoleum, which will bring you back to Palm Drive. Continue along Palm, crossing divided Campus Drive, and, in one block, go right on Museum Way to reach the **Stanford Museum**. It houses mementos of the Stanford family, including the Promontory Point golden spike, as well as an outstanding collection of art. Dating from 1892, it is the oldest museum west of the Mississippi. It withstood the 1906 earthquake because, under Governor Stanford's direction, it had been constructed of concrete reinforced by railroad tracks. Additional sections built after his death, which did not include such reinforcing, were destroyed by the tremor. The museum is open free of charge Tuesday through Friday from 10:00 am to 5:00 pm, Saturday and Sunday from 1:00 to 5:00 pm.

Stanford University

After visiting the museum, return to Palm Drive, and turn again toward the center of campus. Ahead of you, on the far side of the grassy Oval, is the Quadrangle, the heart of the Stanford campus. The sandstone buildings and graceful arches of the Inner Quad date from the time the University opened in 1891, while the Outer Quad was completed in 1903. Walk your bicycle up the ramp to explore this part of campus. Visitor information is found on the left as you enter the Outer Quad.

The most striking architectural feature of the University is **Memorial Church**, located opposite the entrance on the Inner Quad. Although its site was part of the original plans, the church itself was not constructed until after Senator Stanford's death in 1893. Mrs. Stanford then decided it would be built as a memorial to her husband and supervised its completion herself. Dominant features include hand-carved stonework, stained glass windows and magnificent mosaics which cover the exterior facade and interior walls. The non-denominational church was dedicated in 1903. It is open daily to visitors.

Leaving the Quad, you may either ride to see the Red Barn, one of the last remaining buildings of the Stanford Farm, or continue along the main route. It is just over a mile to the barn, part of which is along busy Campus Drive. Whichever way you go, watch out for cyclists if school is in session. There are thousands of bicycles on campus.

*Optional side trip: From the Quad, ride left (away from Hoover Tower) on Serra Street through the barriers. As the road ends, turn right onto Via Palou, then immediately left onto divided Campus Drive West. In about half a mile, turn right on Electioneer Road, named for Senator Stanford's most famous horse. Soon you will see the magnificent Victorian **Red Barn** with its white trim, as well as a bronze horse statue commemorating Electioneer.*

The barn, built in the late 1870's, was only one of the numerous buildings on the Stock Farm. Restored in 1984, it is still used for boarding horses. Located on the road to your right is a white brick stable built in 1892 after a wooden structure burned, killing several horses.

The only other remaining farm building is an old winery. Now converted to shops and called the Stanford Barn, it is located on Quarry Road near the Stanford Shopping Center.

The Stock Farm began to decline after Senator Stanford's death, and its horses were sold off to help the financially troubled university. The Senator's prized ranch officially closed in 1903.

Retrace your route back to the Quad to continue.

Main route continues: Going right on Serra Street from the Quad, you will next come to the Art Gallery, built with funds donated by Senator Stanford's brother Thomas. It was completed in 1917.

Ride through the barriers to **Hoover Tower**. This 285-foot structure, an impressive landmark since 1941, houses the Hoover Institution on War, Revolution and Peace. Its rare collections were begun by Herbert Hoover, president of the United States from 1929 to 1933 and Stanford's most famous alumnus. Hoover memorabilia are exhibited in two rooms on the ground floor, and an observation platform is located at the top. The tower is open daily from 10:00 to 11:45 am and 1:00 to 5:00 pm. (It is closed during Christmas break.)

Continuing along Serra, turn right just past the next structure, the Lou Henry Hoover Building, onto the walkway that cuts through campus. The building to your immediate left is Encina Hall, built as the men's dormitory in 1891 and now used for offices. On your right is the Herbert Hoover Memorial Building, honoring the former president for his humanitarian endeavors and public service.

Ride straight ahead through campus (staying to the left) until the path exits onto the street. This soon becomes Alvarado Row as it angles to the left. In one block you will cross Campus Drive East and enter an area of student residences and faculty houses.

Turning right at the next corner onto Santa Ynez Street, you will shortly begin the only uphill of the ride, about one block long. When the road ends at the top, go left onto Cabrillo Avenue and stop to look at the striking **Lou Henry Hoover House**, surrounded by spacious sloping lawns. The home was built in 1919 after Hoover had been appointed a Stanford trustee. Although the architects were Arthur Clark and his son Birge, Mrs. Hoover contributed greatly to its design. At her death, President Hoover donated the building to the university as a memorial to his wife. It is now the official home of Stanford's presidents.

Continue along Cabrillo for 2 blocks, going left at Mirada Avenue and Gerona Road, and then left again for the downhill along Frenchman's Road. Be sure to notice the red brick Hanna House on top of the hill across the way, a Frank Lloyd Wright design from 1935.

At the bottom of the hill, make a left onto Mayfield Avenue, and when you reach Campus Drive East, go right. There is no shoulder on this busy roadway, so you may wish to ride on the sidewalk. When you reach Escondido Road, turn right towards Escondido Village.

This was formerly the center of Ayrshire Farm, a dairy operation of the larger Matadero Ranch. It was owned by a mysterious Frenchman who used the assumed name Peter Coutts. Once the wealthy editor and publisher of a French newspaper, his liberal political views forced him to leave his country in 1875. His true identity was revealed only after he left California five years later, returning to his homeland. The estate was acquired by Governor Stanford in 1882 and became part of Palo Alto Farm and, later, the university. Today only a few buildings remain of Coutts' once extensive ranch.

Immediately after the barriers, on the left, is the cottage Coutts built in 1875. It became the early home of David Starr Jordan, the university's first president. Today, with numerous additions, it serves as the administrative building of Escondido Village, a complex of student apartments. A short distance further, at #860, is a two-story painted brick structure which was used to house Coutts' library and farm office.

Continue to the end of Escondido and make a left turn onto Stanford Avenue. You have now left the grounds of Stanford University and are riding along the edge of the 1888 development known as College Terrace. It and the nearby town of Mayfield formed the oldest part of what is now the city of Palo Alto.

The Stanfords at first considered Mayfield as the resident village for their university, but insisted it be a dry town. The local inhabitants, however, refused to give up their 13 saloons. Senator Stanford then bought additional land, and established the separate town of Palo Alto, first known as University Park, in 1892. Mayfield gradually faded in importance and was annexed to Palo Alto in 1925.

The history of College Terrace began in 1887 when Alexander Gordon bought 120 acres of farmland and divided it into lots. Since the construction of the new university was already underway, Gordon hoped to attract faculty and fraternities to his development, the nearest private property to the campus. He called it College Terrace, because all of its streets had been named after colleges and universities. It was annexed by neighboring Mayfield in 1891.

Riding along Stanford Avenue, you will see examples of turn-of-the-century cottages typical of the area. Cross congested El Camino Real, continuing on Stanford until it ends at Park Boulevard. A left turn takes you by Peers Park. (Restrooms are located here.) Stay to the right, going through the barriers, onto Mariposa Avenue. At its end, go right onto Churchill, crossing the railroad tracks and busy Alma Street.

In 3 more blocks, turn left, back onto Waverley (following the Bike Route sign). There on the corner, at #1431 Waverley, is the stately Gamble House, built in 1902 for Edwin Percy Gamble, son of the co-founder of Proctor-Gamble Company. It was given to the City of Palo Alto by Gamble's daughter who lived here until her death in 1981. The house and grounds are operated by the Elizabeth Gamble Garden Foundation, which holds gardening classes in the carriage house.

Continue on Waverley, crossing Embarcadero, and make a right onto Melville. Ride on Melville several blocks, crossing Middlefield to reach the Lucie Stern Community Center, a delightful theater and arts complex built around a courtyard. Designed by Birge Clark in 1935, it was a gift from Mrs. Stern to the people of Palo Alto.

From Melville, take the second left onto Guinda Street, following it just over half a mile to University Avenue, where you turn right. Fortunately, this busy street has a bike lane.

The most striking of the numerous large, attractive period homes on this tree-lined street is the **Squire House**, located at #900 on the next corner. It is a perfect example of Classical Revival architecture, a startling innovation in style for Palo Alto when it was built in 1904. Scheduled for demolition in the 1960's, the house was saved by a citizen fundraising drive and is now a State Historical Landmark.

In one block make a right turn onto Hale Street. Then angle left in 2 blocks onto Forest Avenue. Immediately on the left, at #1001 Forest, is a spacious 1895 Victorian. Behind it is the mansion's former carriage house, now a charming private residence. A handsome Queen Anne style home from 1896 is located at #1023.

Continue riding along this street of interesting homes of more recent vintage until it terminates at Center Drive. Go right for several blocks to its end at Channing Avenue. Make a left turn, and then a right at Newell Road. Soon you will come to the Cultural Center, the end of your ride through this attractive university city.

Squire House

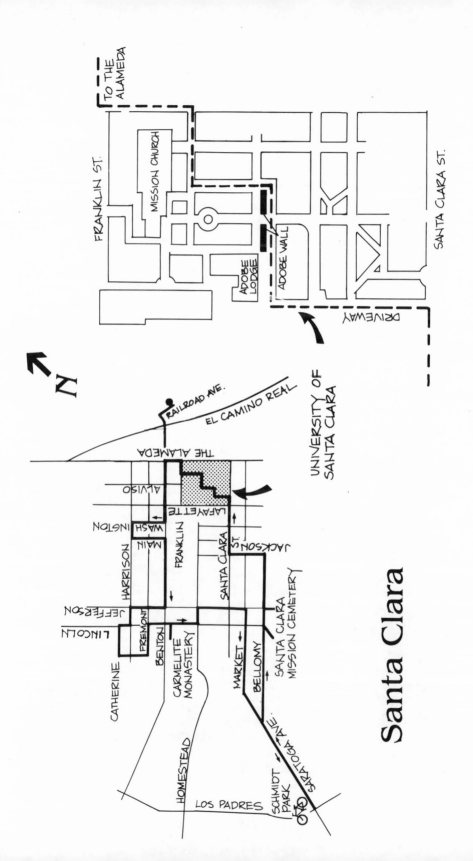

Santa Clara

Santa Clara

Distance: 6 miles

Rating: This short, flat ride is **easy**, following quiet, city streets. Traffic may be occasionally heavy midweek on main roads but is generally light on weekends. It is a pleasant ride for the whole family at any time of year.

Highlights: Santa Clara, incorporated in 1852, is one of the Bay Area's earliest cities and the home of California's first college, now the University of Santa Clara. This ride offers a sampling of Santa Clara's rich heritage, including the Santa Clara Mission, a Carmelite monastery, adobes, Victorians and a pioneer cemetery.

Begin your ride of "The Mission City" at Henry Schmidt Park, located at the intersection of Saratoga Avenue and Los Padres Boulevard. Facilities here include restrooms (closed winter weekends), picnic tables, playground, and tennis courts.

From the park, ride left onto divided Saratoga Avenue. In less than half a mile go straight onto one-way Bellomy Street (Saratoga angles left). As you cross Winchester Boulevard, you will see the **Santa Clara Mission Cemetery** ahead and to the right. At the next corner, Lincoln Street, make a sharp right turn into the entrance of the cemetery, the last resting place of many early Santa Clara Valley pioneers.

The cemetery was established in 1851.when the one near the mission became overcrowded. The chapel here with its copper roof was completed in 1906, and three years later, the cemetery gate was erected in memory of Judge Myles O. O'Connor. O'Connor, who is buried near the chapel, donated the money for O'Connor Sanitarium, now O'Connor Hospital in San Jose.

Other famous names you may recognize as you wander among the tombstones are Pedro de Saisset, the French vice consul in San Jose in whose name the De Saisset Art Museum was established at the University of Santa Clara; Hiram Morgan Hill, founder of the town of Morgan Hill; Martin Murphy, Sr., a major landholder in Santa Clara Valley and father of the founder of Sunnyvale; Maria Soledad Arguello, wife of California's first governor under Mexican rule; and Antonio Suñol, alcalde or mayor of San Jose in 1841.

When you've spent enough time studying tombstones and reading inscriptions, leave the cemetery, turning right on Bellomy. In one block go right again onto Jefferson Street to #373, the Berryessa Adobe. Built in the 1840's on former mission land, this modest dwelling is one of the few early adobes remaining in the valley. Its name derives from the family which purchased it in 1861. The Berryessas were part owners of the New Almaden Quicksilver Mine, but they realized little profit from the mine before selling out their interest.

Returning up Jefferson, take a right, back onto Bellomy. At the barricade, go left on Jackson Street. Continue straight ahead, crossing Market Street at the stop sign. The Spanish-style home on the corner, at #610 Jackson, was built in 1935 for William Wilson, Sr., the founder of the popular Wilson's Jewel Bakery. In one block is Santa Clara Street. Diagonally across the intersection, at #1217 Santa Clara, is a Victorian Gothic cottage, built in 1848 by Andrew Landrum, a local carpenter. It is one of the oldest and best preserved houses in Santa Clara.

Landrum Cottage

Going right on Santa Clara Street, stop in one block at the intersection with Main Street. On the corner, at #714-716 Main, is a large 1886 house that once belonged to Dr. H. H. Warburton. Dr. Warburton is remembered as the town's first physician, settling in Santa Clara in 1848. His original medical office is now part of the San Jose Historical Museum in Kelley Park, but during his later years he maintained his office here at his Main Street home. He continued to practice medicine until his death in 1903 at age 83.

Across the street, at #1085 Santa Clara, is the Arguello house. This stately structure was built about 1860 for the widow and family of Luis Antonio Arguello, the first governor of California under Mexico. Family members continued to live here until 1901. It has since been converted into apartments, but the exterior remains nearly unchanged.

Continue riding along Santa Clara and, just after crossing busy Lafayette Street, turn left at the first driveway. This will take you into the rear of the University of Santa Clara, the location of **Mission Santa Clara de Asis**. Before reaching the end of the driveway, go right onto the sidewalk and down two stairs, walking your bike alongside Adobe Lodge and the length of Adobe Wall into the central yard and gardens. The Mission Church is located on the opposite side of the gardens.

The Santa Clara Mission was established in 1777 near the Guadalupe River, the first of several different locations. The fourth and last mission compound was built in 1822-1825 after earthquakes damaged the previous church and buildings, but it fell into decay following seculari-zation of the mission system in 1836. In 1851, at the request of the Bishop of California, the Jesuits founded Santa Clara College in the old mission buildings. Thus was established California's first institution of higher education. The college was granted a university charter in 1855 and has maintained a long history as one of the top-ranked Catholic institutions in the country.

Little remains of the 1822 mission compound except the Old Adobe Wall and Adobe Lodge, once the granary storehouse and now the remodeled Faculty Club. In 1926 fire destroyed the church, and the present replica was constructed in 1929. The mission church is open daily to visitors.

Also on campus is the De Saisset Art Gallery and Museum, which houses a collection of early California and mission artifacts. Located near the main entrance to the university, it is open free of charge Tuesday through Friday, from 10:00 am to 5:00 pm, Saturday and Sunday from 1:00 to 5:00 pm.

Leave the university by the north side entrance, being careful to avoid the spikes in the roadway. A right turn takes you onto Franklin Street. Don't miss the two brightly painted cottages on the left, now in use as offices. At the traffic light, turn left onto The Alameda. Once lined with trees planted by the padres in 1799, The Alameda was the road leading from the mission to the Pueblo of San Jose.

Stop in half a block to see the **Woman's Club Adobe** at #3260, on the right, built about 1790. The sole survivor of the third mission compound, it was probably an apartment for Indian families. Don Jose Peña received this building in 1840, along with several others, as part of his land grants. It remained in the family until acquired by the Santa

Clara Women's Club and dedicated as their headquarters in 1914. It is a State Registered Landmark.

At the next corner, make a right turn onto Benton Street. Just after crossing El Camino, you will come to the Santa Clara Railroad Station, the oldest operating passenger station west of the Mississippi. It dates from 1863 and has been restored by the South Bay Historical Railroad Society. Inside is a small museum of railroad artifacts and photographs.

Return on Benton and cross The Alameda. As you ride by Alviso Street on the left, notice the large false-front building down the block. Built in the 1870's as the Santa Clara Verein, this simple structure served as the cultural and social center for the once powerful local German community. Forerunner of the modern day health club, it also sponsored gymnastic events, and its members included some of the town's most influential citizens.

Turn right in 2 blocks at Washington Street to a neighborhood of historic homes. On the corner, at #1116, is an unrestored house built in 1897 for Dr. Judson Paul. In marked contrast are two other residences of note along this street. #1184 was built in 1861 by Santa Clara pioneer carpenter Calvin Russell. Across the street, at #1179, is the lovely Franck house, constructed in 1905 and originally owned by the son of Senator Frederic Franck.

Morse Mansion

At the corner of Washington and Fremont (#981 Fremont) is the magnificent **Morse Mansion**, an elaborate Queen Anne style house dating from 1892. Charles Copeland Morse was the founder of the seed business which eventually became the Ferry-Morse Seed Company. Thus, this wonderful building is known as "the house that seeds built." Be sure to notice the old carriage house in back.

Continue on Washington to the next corner, turning left onto Harrison Street to discover a block of well-maintained houses typical of the late 19th century. Of special interest is the red house at #1051, built in 1891. It is a fine example of "wedding cake" Victorian architecture.

In another block, go left again onto Main Street to see more of Santa Clara's old homes. #1206, the Miller house, was built in 1874 for the store keeper of the New Almaden Mine. Across the street, at #1091 Fremont, is an 1868 dwelling that was later owned by Franklin Hichborn, an important journalist and political writer in the early part of the century. The well-kept Johnson house is located in the next block, at #1159 Main. It was constructed in the 1850's of precut lumber shipped around Cape Horn from Maine.

At the corner on the left, at #1075 Benton, you will find the house of Dr. Arthur Saxe, the health officer during the smallpox epidemic of 1873. Just beyond was his office, located at #1045. These buildings date from the 1850's. From Main, go right onto Benton. At #1191 on the next corner is a Queen Anne style house built for the Robert Menzel family in 1895. Menzel was a high-ranking city official for many years.

Continue on Benton for 3 more blocks, turning right on Jefferson Street. Across from the park, at #1210, is the New England style home built in the 1850's for R. L. Higgins, a San Jose real estate developer.

One block further along, go left onto Harrison Street, turning right at Lincoln and left in one block onto Catherine Street. On the corner, at #1380 Lincoln, is a charming home dating from 1897, constructed by John Morgan for his niece. Originally three levels, the house was lowered in the 1920's, eliminating seven rooms downstairs. In 2 blocks, turn left onto Pierce, noting the unusual house on the corner, at #1768 Catherine. In 2 more short blocks, take a left onto Fremont where you will pass #1756, a small Pioneer-style home from the 1870's. Originally it had two stories, but one was removed in 1924 when the building was moved to this location. At the corner, take a right back onto Lincoln.

As you cross Benton, you will notice the pink plaster walls of the **Carmelite Monastery**. Turn right into the entrance, and pedal down the tree-lined driveway of the monastery, a quiet and peaceful place to pause.

This land, once known as New Park, was part of a 96-acre ranch. Judge Hiram Bond, a self-made millionaire from New York, bought the estate in 1895. Jack London, who knew the Bond sons from his days of Klondike gold mining, was a frequent visitor. The ranch was supposedly used as one of the settings in London's *Call of the Wild*, and the Bonds' dog is reputed to be the model for Buck.

In 1905 Judge Bond suffered financial reverses, and New Park was put up for sale. The property was finally purchased in 1913 by Senator James Phelan, owner of Villa Montalvo in Saratoga, in order to establish a Carmelite monastery in memory of his sister, Alice Phelan Sullivan. Alice is buried in the ornate chapel. This structure, erected in 1917, is considered to be the most perfect example of Spanish Renaissance ecclesiastical architecture in the New World.

Although there are nuns in residence here, you will not encounter any as you explore the grounds. This is because Carmelite nuns are a cloistered order, living in silence and solitude, devoting their lives to prayer and meditation. Only a few are allowed to be seen in public or to leave the monastery.

Evidence of the old Bond ranch may still be seen in the gardens, the carriage house (where the nuns now live), and the tank house. The main house, however, was razed in 1916 to make room for the chapel.

The monastery grounds are open daily from 6:30 am to 4:30 pm, Sunday from 8:00 am to 5:00 pm. The chapel is usually closed except for services (Sunday Mass is at 10:30 am), but you may ask to have it opened in order to see the inside of this beautiful little building.

Harris-Lass House

As you leave the cool, pleasant monastery grounds, continue right on Lincoln. In 2 blocks, turn left on Homestead. There you can admire the large Italianate style house on the corner, #1588. It was once owned by William Kiely, Sr., Santa Clara mayor. Continue on Homestead for one block, turning right on Jefferson. In 3 blocks, make a right onto Market, following the one-way across Winchester Boulevard.

In the next block, make one last stop, at #1889 Market, the **Harris-Lass House**. This Italianate style home was built in 1865 for Henry Harris and his family. In 1906 it was purchased by Captain Lass, a retired sea captain, and members of his family continued to live here until 1985. It is now owned by the city and has been designated a Historic Preserve as the last remaining farmstead in Santa Clara.

To return to your starting point, continue along Market, which immediately becomes Saratoga. Follow it back to the park, and you will have completed your tour of the delightful old homes and buildings which make up historic Santa Clara.

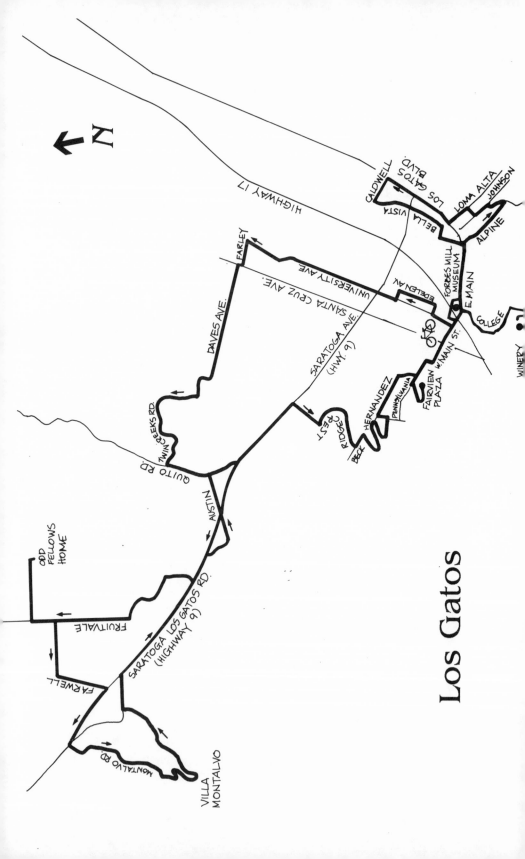

Los Gatos

Los Gatos

Distance: 12 miles with 7 mile optional side trip

Rating: This ride and its optional side trip are **moderately strenuous**, as there are several gradual to demanding climbs. None is very long, however. Traffic may be heavy and fast-moving on Highway 9, but there is a good shoulder. Be aware, too, that downtown Los Gatos can be congested, especially on a summer weekend.

Highlights: Late 19th century homes abound in Los Gatos, ranging from charming cottages to fine mansions. Many have been beautifully restored. The town's heritage is also reflected in some interesting turn-of-the-century commercial buildings. As a bonus, this ride offers visits to two museums, the old Novitiate Winery, and an optional side trip to Villa Montalvo in Saratoga.

The origins of Los Gatos date back to the 1850's when James Alexander Forbes built a flour mill along Los Gatos Creek on land that was once part of Rancho Rinconada de los Gatos. The mill became the focal point of a tiny community called Forbes Mill at first, and later, Forbestown. The coming of the railroad in 1878 established Forbestown as a lumber center, soon renamed Los Gatos. The building boom which followed resulted in many of the lovely Victorian homes you can see today.

Begin your ride at Old Town, a popular complex of shops and restaurants built around a 1925 stucco schoolhouse. Old Town is located on University Avenue just off Main Street in the center of Los Gatos. There is a large parking lot across the street and public restrooms can be found near the bell tower of the Old Town Theater.

From Old Town, ride right toward Highway 9 on University Avenue, a busy street with many pretty 19th century Victorian homes. In 2 blocks, another right brings you onto Miles. At the next corner, on the right, are two especially notable homes. #129 Edelen Avenue is a dignified 1890 Queen Anne style residence with a fine carriage house. Across the street is #130, which features a curved porch and shingled tower. It dates from 1886.

Turn left on Edelen, following the road as it curves onto Bentley Avenue. This brings you back to University Avenue where you go right. Of special interest here is the **Honeymoon House** at #315 University. It was built by Harry Perrin in 1896 for his bride, and is a rare example of the Victorian Romanesque style of architecture used for a private residence, rather than a public building.

Honeymoon House

Continue along University, riding through the busy intersection with Saratoga Avenue (Highway 9). Don't miss the fine Victorian on the left at #425 University. Soon you will come to the intersection with Blossom Hill Road. The entrance to popular Lake Vasona County Park is down the hill to your right.

Ride straight ahead on University, taking the second left turn onto Farley Road (following the Bike Route sign). In one block is Santa Cruz Avenue, where you make a right turn, and then immediately go left on Daves Avenue. The second house on the left, #17560 Daves, dates from 1873. It was built by John Daves who crossed the plains to Santa Clara Valley with his parents in 1852. He had a 500 acre farm here.

Another historic dwelling is located at the end of Top of the Hill, an unmarked narrow road just opposite Kirkorian Way, less than half a mile further along. This house was built in 1890 by a retired seaman. Later owners, the Hitts, installed a pipe organ in the water tower and held church services in the barn. Hitt ordained himself a minister and called his church group "Hittites." The Hitts also manufactured fireworks here until World War II, when they switched to rodent bombs. This interesting set of buildings is located on private property.

Continue riding on Daves Avenue and, just before the road goes left and downhill, turn right at the stop sign onto Via Caballero (at the Bike Route sign). As the street curves left, it becomes Twin Creeks Road. This part of Los Gatos has many lovely, newer homes. When the road ends, take a left at Quito Road, named for the rancho located here in the 1840's. Traffic on this narrow road may be fast-moving and there is little shoulder, so use caution.

In a quarter mile, you will come to the intersection with Austin Way, the location of the once busy settlement of Austin Corners. All that remains today is an old garage, and tracks of the Peninsula Railway, an interurban electric line that ran from San Jose to Palo Alto in the early part of the century. The Los Gatos-Saratoga Wine and Fruit Company was also situated here from 1885 until the building was razed in 1919.

If you are doing the 7 mile optional side trip to Villa Montalvo, turn right on Austin Way. If you are heading back to Los Gatos, continue on Quito until it ends at Saratoga-Los Gatos Road (Highway 9), and go left at the traffic signal.

Optional side trip: *Ride on Austin Way, going right when it joins Saratoga-Los Gatos Road. You will have a gradual uphill for about half a mile. To get away from this noisy highway, take the second right onto Via Colina, then the first left at Monte Vista Drive, and another left on Valle Vista. This will bring you to Fruitvale Avenue, where you go right toward West Valley College.*

Just after the road divides you will come to the entrance to the Odd Fellows Home for the Aged next to San Marcos Road. A right turn will bring you to the impressive 1912 Mission-Revival style main building. John McLaren, who landscaped Golden Gate Park, was a member of the I.O.O.F. and designed the gardens here. The grounds are very peaceful and offer a brief escape from traffic.

*To continue on your way, pedal back to Fruitvale, turning left. Take the first right onto Farwell Avenue, which brings you back to Highway 9. Here you go right, heading toward **Villa Montalvo**. In less than half a mile, make a left at Montalvo Road, using the left turn lane.*

Montalvo Road was once the long driveway to the mansion, the entrance to the estate being marked by the pillars still found here. Ride one mile up Montalvo Road; there is a short, steep hill just past the Arboretum Center. At the end of the road you will find the stately building that was once the home of James D. Phelan, three-time mayor of San Francisco and United States Senator.

Villa Montalvo

This 19-room Mediterranean style villa was completed in 1914, just before Phelan began his term as senator. No expense was spared; the main doors came from a Spanish palace, the rooms were filled with priceless works of art, and the gardens were laid out by John McLaren. Once the scene of many a lavish party, Villa Montalvo is now an art gallery and cultural center, as specified in Phelan's will. It is open Thursday and Friday from 1:00 to 4:00 pm, Saturday and Sunday from 11:00 am to 4:00 pm. The grounds are maintained by the county as an arboretum and are open daily from 9:00 am to 5:00 pm.

After exploring the house and grounds, bicycle down the one-way exit, which becomes Piedmont Road, turning right when it ends at Mendelsohn Lane. Turn right again at Saratoga-Los Gatos Road, heading back to Los Gatos.

In about a mile, in the middle of a gradual downhill, angle right onto Austin Way. A section of this road is paved with brick and was part of the original Saratoga-Los Gatos Road. The old Austin School, built in 1912, is located at #19010.

Continuing on Austin Way brings you back to Highway 9. At this intersection is La Hacienda, a large inn and restaurant. In 1902 the Nippon Mura Inn was developed here as a resort for San Franciscans. The buildings were modified Japanese traditional style, and one of these has been incorporated into the present structure. The inn was part of the town of Austin Corners. Shortly after passing La Hacienda, you rejoin the main route.

Main route continues: Soon you will enter the town of Monte Sereno. Just as the road begins to narrow, turn right onto Ridgecrest. After a short, stiff climb, the street ends at Beck Avenue. Go left, then follow the road as it curves right downhill along the wooded canyon on Hernandez Avenue. At the first intersection, turn right on Chestnut, then in one block left on Overlook Road. Stop at #18000, on the right, where the large eucalyptus trees line the street.

This was an estate called La Estancia. The house, built in 1900, is an excellent example of Mission Revival architecture, but is particularly interesting because of its method of construction. The owners wanted to incorporate the original 1880's ranch house into their new, larger home, and so the contractor had it cut in half and pulled apart by teams of horses. A center section was built to join the two halves.

Continue down Overlook, turning left on Wissahickon Avenue and then right back onto Hernandez. Interesting large old homes are all around, just waiting to be admired, so take your time on the downhill.

When the street ends, go right onto Glen Ridge Avenue. Here again are many fine period homes. At the corner turn right on Pennsylvania, and in one block, left up Fairview Avenue. At the top of a short, steep climb, go left on **Fairview Plaza** to see a group of charming late 19th century homes built around a landscaped center island. This example of an early housing development is a designated Historic District.

Retrace your route down the hill, turning right on Pennsylvania, right on Bayview, and then left onto West Main Street.

At the next intersection, on Tait Avenue, is the Los Gatos Museum, located in a former firehouse. The museum has an interesting history section displaying items of local and general interest. It is open free of charge Tuesday through Sunday, from 10:00 am to 4:00 pm.

Continue along West Main, and in 2 blocks you will reach Santa Cruz Avenue. This street, with its colorful variety of shops and restaurants, is the heart of downtown Los Gatos. The traffic may be heavy here, so use caution. Cross Santa Cruz Avenue, using the right lane, and pause at the Town Plaza, once a stagecoach stop.

At one time Santa Cruz Avenue was a toll road with a gate and toll house located a few blocks up the street toward the hills. The Santa Cruz Road was the only way to transport felled redwoods from the mountains to the mills and markets in the valley. From 1857 to 1877, haulers were charged from 50¢ for a two-horse team to $1 for a six-horse team. The road was made public after the high tolls caused a revolt among the haulers.

From the Plaza you can see several turn-of-the-century commercial structures. On the corner diagonal from the Plaza is La Cañada Building, a local landmark constructed in 1894. Its most notable feature is the candle-snuffer turret. Across from the Plaza on Main Street, are an old bank and opera house.

The Plaza itself is a pleasant place to relax, fill your water bottle, or have a picnic. Here you may also view a 200-pound firebell from 1899, used to summon volunteer firemen and toll curfew. When you are ready, continue on Main Street through this busy part of town.

Just on the other side of the Highway 17 bridge you will pass the entrance to the Los Gatos Creek Trail, a 1.8 mile dirt and gravel road leading to the dam at Lexington Reservoir.

At the next corner, turn right at College Avenue. Notice the intricate use of bricks in the wall paralleling College. The wall was constructed in 1910 as part of the Mariotti Saloon and Hotel which once stood here. College Avenue leads to the Marion Winery (formerly the Novitiate Winery), a moderately steep climb of less than a mile into the foothills of the Santa Cruz Mountains.

Ride up College, enjoying the wooded hillsides, and in just over half a mile, turn right into the property of the Domaine M. **Marion Winery**. Continue uphill to the winery buildings.

The land here was purchased by the Jesuits in 1886 for a retreat. A winery was established two years later and operated as the Novitiate Winery until 1986. The operation is now under control of Marion and Company, a Saratoga-based vintner. Although few of the early buildings remain, some of the old equipment has been preserved. The tasting room is open daily from 11:00 am to 4:30 pm. (During winter months, it is open only Wednesday through Sunday.) The terrace is an enjoyable place to picnic, and restrooms are available nearby.

Although the Jesuits are no longer connected with the winery, they continue to maintain a retirement residence for priests in the large white building that can be seen further up the hill.

After enjoying views of the valley below, retrace your route back down College, turning right on East Main.

Notice the interesting hotel and red brick buildings from the 1890's located on the left. A short distance further on, just as East Main begins to head uphill, turn right on Alpine Avenue. Immediately turn right again, staying on Alpine.

Ride to #75, a large, well-restored house from 1885. This was the Moser home, and Sarah Winchester, a friend of Mrs. Moser, was said to be a frequent visitor. At the end of Alpine, go left for a downhill along Foster Road. This brings you to Johnson Avenue, where you will see some charming Victorian-era cottages. Turn left on Johnson, right on Cross Way, and then left again on Loma Alta Avenue.

The modest 1894 house at #110 belonged to Zephyr Macabee, who invented the Macabee gopher trap in 1900. This invention was hailed by Santa Clara Valley orchardists, and by the mid-1920's, 1000 traps were being produced here each day. The company continues to operate at this location.

Loma Alta ends at Los Gatos Boulevard (the continuation of Main Street). Before turning right, be sure to notice the house across the street at #49. This home was built around 1875 by Peter Johnson and is considered to be one of the most important early residences in Los Gatos, having undergone little structural change in over 100 years.

Los Gatos Boulevard is the location of many more lovely Victorians. Traffic may be heavy here, but there is a bike lane. A nicely restored large cottage, at #122, on the next corner was once the summer home of Alma Spreckels of San Francisco. Across the street, at #207, is an impressive Italianate style house from about 1890.

Continuing along Los Gatos Boulevard, pass Saratoga Avenue and ride to the next traffic light. The street on the right is Kennedy, but you will go left onto Caldwell Avenue.

Turn left again on Bella Vista Avenue. This will take you away from the traffic for a bit, as you make your way back to the main part of town. Bella Vista crosses over Highway 9 and becomes New York Avenue on the downhill. Go left on Pleasant Street (following the Bike Route signs) and then right on East Main.

You will again ride past the 1924 Neo-classical style high school, whose alumni include actresses Olivia de Havilland and her sister Joan Fontaine. One block past the school, make a right turn onto Church Street toward the **Forbes Mill Museum**. When Church curves to the right, go straight ahead instead and down the hill to the left. The museum is housed in an 1880 annex building, all that remains of the four-story Forbes flour mill. This is where the town of Los Gatos originated. After serving a variety of uses over the years, the annex has been renovated into a regional museum dedicated to preserving the heritage of the Santa Clara Valley. It is open free of charge Tuesday through Sunday, from 10:00 am to 4:00 pm. (Another entrance to the Los Gatos Creek trail is located behind the museum.)

From the museum, walk your bike over the footbridge above Highway 17 to the lower level of Old Town. Go to the left and exit through a parking lot, riding down Lundy Lane to Main Street. Make a right onto Main and immediately turn right again on University. Note the decorative arches on the 1906 stone Fretwell Building on the corner.

This brings you back to the main entrance to Old Town where you began your tour of Los Gatos, one of the most charming towns in the Bay Area.

Acknowledgements

Many people have contributed to this book. Bud O'Hare, Pete Blasberg and Bev Fritsch helped with route planning and bicycled the rides with me. Nancy Olsen played a major role in the development of the book and took on the task of final editing, despite her own busy schedule. The cover design, maps and layout are by Susan Cronin-Paris, who brought her considerable talents and enthusiastic support to the project. Kathleen Hallam edited the manuscript, offering valuable comments. The final copy was proof-read by Harry Wessenberg and Beth and John Stearns. Helpful suggestions and encouragement were provided by my friends and fellow cyclists in the Western Wheelers Bicycle Club. And many citizens eagerly shared information about the unique history of their towns. To everyone who helped make this book a reality, my deepest appreciation.

Photo Credits

All photographs are by the author except for the following: Betty Johnston, pages 1, 20, 22, 50, 77, 78, 82, 102, 120, 123, 162; Bud O'Hare, pages 25, 90. Photographs provided courtesy of John Muir Historic Site, National Park Service, page 65; Livermore Area Recreation and Park District, page 86; East Bay Regional Park District, page 92.

How to Order Additional Books

Additional copies of *A Bicyclist's Guide to Bay Area History* may be ordered from the publisher. Send $8.95 plus $2.00 for shipping and California sales tax to Fair Oaks Publishing Company, 941 Populus Place, Sunnyvale, CA 94086.